CONCILIUM

Religion in the Seventies

CONCILIUM

Concilium 130 (10/1979): Moral Theology

THE DIGNITY
OF THE
DESPISED OF
THE EARTH

Edited by

Jacques Pohier
and
Dietmar Mieth

THE SEABURY PRESS/NEW YORK

1979
The Seabury Press, 815 Second Avenue, New York, N.Y. 10017
ISBN: 0-8164-2038-6 (pbk.)   0-8164-0131-4

T. & T. Clark Ltd., 36 George Street, Edinburgh EH2 2LQ
ISBN: 0-567-30010-2 (pbk.)

Library of Congress Catalog Card Number: 80-65212
Printed in the United States of America

CONTENTS

Part III
Present Christian Practice of 'Neither Jew nor Greek, neither slave nor free, neither male nor female'

Part IV
The Worth of God and the Worth of the 'Worthless'

Editorial

THERE is more and more talk of theolog*ies* of the New Testament and even of Christolog*ies* of the New Testament, in the plural, with the emphasis on their variety, let alone the divergences between them. They do, however, agree on numerous points and one of the points of agreement is all the more significant for bearing on an aspect of the ministry and behaviour of Jesus which was as bewildering for his disciples as for his detractors. This concerns the way Jesus treated the men and women whom the civil and religious society of his time considered unworthy of the salvation of God and of the attention of his messenger. The way Jesus behaved with sinners and all those whom society and religion rejected or excluded earned him the reprobation of those who thought that they were the keepers of moral civil and religious worthiness and who jealously guarded respect for it down to the minutest detail. The fact that Jesus wanted to put those who by rights belonged to the lowest rank in the first rank was one of the reasons why he was put to death, because this was as blasphemous as what he said about God.

The point is that the way Jesus behaved towards the 'unworthy' was not just the expression of an exceptional generosity or philanthropy; no, it was simply that Jesus wanted sinners and the poor to enjoy the inherent worth which he perceived that his God recognised they had. For Jesus it is by coming to appreciate the worth of the 'worthless' that we come to appreciate the true worth of the Father. This is what those who always claim to know more about God and about man because they occupy the most respectable religious and social positions did not forgive him. This is what Paul understood when he turned the typical Pharisee's problem inside out in a way that is as important as his doctrine of justification by faith or of the gratuitousness of salvation (although all these doctrines in fact spring from his having first turned his understanding of God inside out): 'There is neither Jew nor Greek, there is neither slave nor free, there is neither male nor female, for you are all one in Christ Jesus' (Gal. 3:28).

This is why the worth of the unworthy is no small part of Christian morality just as the fact that we come to appreciate the worth of God by appreciating the worth of the worthless is no small part of the revelation of God by and in Jesus Christ. And by the same token it is no small part of believers' fidelity to their Lord; on the contrary, it is a touchstone of the authenticity with which the communion of believers, the Church, allows itself to be directed by the Spirit of its Lord and to follow in his footsteps.

It is easy enough to agree to all this at the level of declaration of principle on paper or on the public platform. The fact is, however, that all the economic and cultural—and even the religious—mechanisms of our society prevent the worth of the worthless from being recognised. The chief places are well guarded and there is not much room at the top. Following Jesus Christ in this way obliges us to fight against all the powers of the world, in the Johannine and Pauline sense of this expression—and sometimes even to die, as Jesus himself had to. It is no use invoking the name of Jesus unless we are faithful on this point. And on this point where do we stand, fellow Christians, where do we stand?

The purpose of this issue of *Concilium* is not to open a discussion nor to draw up a balance sheet on this point. The study of twenty centuries of Christianity would produce a picture featuring both fidelities and infidelities. The same goes for the attitudes of churches today. Our purpose is more immediate: we want to reinvigorate and to illumine the will of believers to live in the same Spirit as the Lord on this point.

There is, however, a trap here which it is difficult to avoid. Mgr. Francisco Claver makes the point very vigorously in his article: people talk about the worth of the worthless as if their worth were something they have not yet acquired and which somehow had to be given them. And the corollary of this is that those who do already possess this worth should be prepared to share it compassionately with those who are deprived of it. But this is not how the worth of the worthless is, or should be, in Christianity. They have already got this worth, and they have it by right and on principle, or rather from God. It is because God is the sort of God who acknowledges the worth of those said to be worthless that they possess this worth. It is not a question of giving it to them, and those who think of themselves as worthy have nothing to give them. On the contrary, they have to fight against everything inside and outside themselves that prevents them from recognising in others the worth which they refuse them. Their task is not to grant worth to the worthless, but to recognise it where it already is, to allow it to express itself, to open the door to it, to serve it.

It follows that in order to deal with the question of the worth of the worthless in a properly theological way, we have to make an epistemological choice, based upon the very nature of the subject. It is not those who seem to be most worthy whom we must ask to deal with this subject, but those who belong to the world of the worthless in some way or other. Our aim has, therefore, been, wherever possible, to have the various articles written by people belonging to the different categories of the worthless we are dealing with. It is in this way that the article on the Church and the poor in Latin America is written by a Latin American whom the poor on that continent think of as their brother, and we are proud and glad that he happens also to be a bishop (Mgr. Leonidas Proaño). The article on the Church's position in regard to women is written oy a woman (Donna Singles). The articles on the attitude of Christian communities towards ethnic minorities is written by a member of an ethnic minority in the Philippines the members of which have to fight for the recognition of the dignity of their 'tribes', and to fight to the point of being persecuted by a majority which is nevertheless Catholic; and here again we Christians are proud and glad that the spokesman is again a bishop (Mgr. Francisco Claver). The article on Christians and societies based on a caste system is written by an Indian born in such a system (Mariasusai Dhavamony). The article on the attitude of the wealthy societies of the West towards migrants is written by two immigrants who concern themselves with this problem in the Christian country which is richest at once in material goods and in immigrants—the U.S.A. (Gianfausto Rosoli and Lydio Tomasi). And the article on the relationships between 'worthy' and 'unworthy' churches is written by an African Christian (Meinrad Hebga).

This epistemological option is, however, not confined to articles in which we wanted to suggest some aspects of current Christian application of the Pauline axiom 'Neither Jew nor Greek, neither slave nor free, neither male nor female'. It also applies to articles that seem to be purely historical or exegetic or theoretical. The fact is that the way one speaks of these things varies according to the side of the fence on which one happens to find oneself. So here again we wanted to give the right of speech to authors who were in one way or another on the same side as the worthless ones about whom they were writing. Thus the article on the attitude of Christians in the middle ages (or, to be precise, in the pivotal period of the eleventh century) is written, not by a Christian, but by a Jew who also happens to have an international reputation as a scholar. The article on the attitude of Christians towards the 'savages' at the time of the colonisation of America is written by an Argentinian, who is as well known for his scholarly competence as for his commitment to the theory and practice of the theology of liberation (Enrique Dussel). Charles Pietri can hardly be faulted for not being a slave of antiquity but nobody can deny that, in the absence of a slave, we could not find anybody more competent to deal with the attitude of ancient Christianity towards slaves. And as for the behaviour of Jesus towards the poor and the outcast, and the quite fundamental importance of this for subsequent Christian morality, we are proud and glad to have an article written by an exegete who comes from a country where the Church—the Church as a whole: layfolk, religious men and women, priests and bishops—is persecuted on account of its defence of the 'worthless' (Jon Sobrino).

The difficulties we have encountered in gathering a group of authors inhabiting the five continents of the world have compelled us to abandon in two cases the methodological choice we have made. Our readers will not be sorry since they will as a result be able to benefit from the expertise of Enzo Bianchi who shows us that the originality of the God of the Old Testament was responsible for the correspondingly original status of the 'worthless'. And Jost Eckert shows very well how difficult the first Christian communities found it to practise the teaching of Jesus: the 'marvellous unity' of the first community of legend is badly in need of serious demythologisation. As for Enda McDonagh, friendship and tact forbid us to mention more than one of the qualifications which entitle him to speak about the worth alike of God and of the worthless: he happens to belong to a community riven by conflicts in which Christianity is, unhappily, invoked on both sides.

As we have already said, we do not intend to draw up a critical dossier, whether positive or negative, about the fidelity to the Spirit and to the example of their Lord in regard to the worthless on the part of the Church as institution or believers down the ages. At the same time we cannot help asking what sort of image of the Church and of Christians emerges from the different articles in this issue. And if one does ask this question, then the image that finally emerges is the Gospel image of the field of wheat and tares. The middle ages witnesses the terrible persecution of 1096, but in the midst of it Johann, Bishop of Speyer, wants to protect the refugees 'as a father protects his child'. The sixteenth century has Sepúlveda, but it also has Las Casas. Mgr. Proaño does not hesitate to say that in Latin America today there are two churches: the rich church allied to the powers that be and the other that has identified itself with the poor. Mgr. Claver tells us about the courageous—and dangerous—struggle of the Christian communities of the ethnic minorities in the Philippines, and M. Dhavamony shows that some Christian communities in India occasionally allow themselves to be contaminated by the caste system which they purport to condemn. G. Rosoli and L. Tomasi inform us of the considerable effort being made on behalf of minorities by the Holy See and conferences of bishops, but it goes without saying that these appeals would be unnecessary if believers in the local churches were already opening their doors to immigrants. The wheat and the tares. . . . We are reminded that it is not our business to sort them out from each other. But we are also warned that each one of us should do his best to cultivate his own patch and to sow good grain in it.

It is in this spirit that we shall conclude by concerning ourselves with our own patch, *Concilium* itself. *Concilium* is a review got up by 'worthy' theologians of the 'worthy' churches (which is not to say that they have never suffered indignities or always dissociated themselves from such unworthy activities). But the churches of Asia, Africa and Latin America are now asking not to be treated any longer as so many theological colonies of Europe and North America. *Concilium* was born out of Vatican II and took its name from an experience which its founders shared. Two years ago our editorial committee joined certain theologians from North America to put the question: Do we need a new Council, Vatican III?

Whatever the reply be, one thing is certain: the 'worthless' must refind the voice to which God himself gives them the right. They must refind the place in the Church that is their due: the first. How long will we have to wait for a Council of the worthless? Would that not be a truly ecumenical Council at last? If, by tackling this subject today and by making the methodological choice which flowed from it, *Concilium* were, however modestly, helping the worthless in the Church to speak out in such a way and the Church itself to become a permanent council of the 'worthless', our review would not be completely unworthy of the fine name it bears.

Translated by John Maxwell

Part I

The Biblical Data

Enzo Bianchi

The Status of Those without Dignity in the Old Testament

IN THE last few decades social conscience and social responsibility among Christians have undoubtedly been growing. This has led to the elaboration of 'political theologies' and 'theologies of revolution'. It is therefore natural that all this should have had an effect upon our reading and interpretation of the Bible, and that the exploration of the Scriptures should have shifted its attention to the social structures and relationships obtaining among God's people of the first covenant and in the New Testament Church. The proclamation of the evangelical message, as it gradually becomes purer, bolder and clearer, is identified with proclamation from the cross and the liberation emanating therefrom. The cross signifies poverty, spoliation, radical humiliation, in order that wordly wisdom might be repudiated and the wisdom of God revealed (1Cor. 1:17 and 2:5). Those sections of the community 'without dignity', the poor, the oppressed, appear for the first time, as of right, as the most important beneficiaries of the message of liberation. They had found defence and protection in the prophets and in the social enactments of the Jewish people. They could identify with Jesus of Nazareth, who not only acted to help people 'without dignity', but desired to be totally at one with them. Jesus, in fact, rejected wealth in favour of poverty, form and dignity, in favour of formlessness and slavery! (2 Cor. 8:9 and Phil. 2:6 ff.) Our inquiry, therefore, moves over well-explored territory,[1] and shows how, even in a nationalistic perspective, where the social structures are rigid, a status for those who were 'without dignity in Israel' might be found. Most importantly, we should like to show that, underlying the law there is a revelation, that morality is transcended by theology, that ethics, too, becomes prophecy in the very heart of the ancient alliance.[2]

3

The whole of Scripture evidences an interest in, and observation of, those people whose state is not one of dignity, and who are present in the land of Israel. They might be slaves (*ebed*), foreign immigrants (*gher*), mean or wretched (*misken* and *jelka*), men of whom one is ashamed (*Ras*), weak (*dal*), hunch-backed (*anaw*), oppressed (*ebyon*) or the individual who can only answer 'yes' to his master (*ani*). All these however, find a figure which represents them all in the state of being 'without dignity', and who does so perfectly: the '*ebed IHWH*', the servant Messiah, who is simultaneously historical and prophetic; and who at the same time is also an individual in the history of salvation and a collective figure.

1. THE SERVANT OF IHWH AS THE PERFECT EXAMPLE OF AN INDIVIDUAL
WITHOUT DIGNITY

In the prophecy of Isaiah, the figure of the servant of IHWH emerges in the noted four odes in a growing revelation. Presented as chosen, and defined as servant (Isa. 42:1-4) he is given the task of taking the divine right (*mispat*) and law (*torah*) to the nations. His audience is to be the whole of humanity, but his mission is a failure (Isa. 49:1-6). Yet it is he who, at a high personal price, is to raise the oppressed and those whose dignity is not recognised (Isa. 50:4-9), until he becomes the just man who suffers, the individual without form, the most perfectly alienated person, the negative man (Isa. 52:13-53, 12). Above all, in the last ode, he is described as thing, *res*, a total slave, truly exhibiting all the characteristics of the 'negative man' outlined by the Frankfurt School.

This servant of IHWH is acutely aware of social evils, bears the entire weight thereof, and desires to liberate his people therefrom. His attempt, however, is not only ineffective, but fills him with anguish (Isa. 3:4).

Considered negatively by the society around him, he is scorned, derided and expelled. What he does is easily used against him (Isa. 49:4), with the result that, in the eyes of people who matter, he is considered inept and useless, as acting against the common good (Isa. 53:7).

God, without a doubt, is far from him (Isa. 53:4) and he must therefore be removed (Isa. 53:5). Without form or dignity, (Isa. 53:2); he becomes voiceless during the trial against him (Isa. 53:7); and put to death not only physically, but also socially, psychologically and from a religious standpoint; he perceives that he will long be remembered along with evildoers (Isa. 53:8-9). He is a man who clashes with the worldly mentality, who gives up his life to help all other men (Isa. 53:10-12). In the service of his people, right up to the end he is accused of effrontery (Isa. 50:7), and yet he is aware that his right is to be near the Lord (Isa. 50:8-9). He knows also that he is addressing himself to those who have lost faith (Isa. 50:4): some of these obtain liberation and salvation, others become aware of their state of servitude and take the first steps towards becoming liberators themselves (Isa. 53:10-12).[3]

This figure is the best example of a person 'without dignity' in the Old Testament, and he undoubtedly illustrates the place that all such people have in the economy of salvation. This seems to be hermeneutic space where three readings of history intersect: the collective reading of Israel without dignity within universal history; the Christian prophetic reading which sees in Jesus of Nazareth, the person who, from having had the dignity of God, became a nonentity (a person without dignity); and the reading of the negative man, the oppressed, the foreigner, the alienated person, who by their very presence testify to the fact that God will bring about justice by promising that those who have no dignity that they will attain the highest dignity through liberation.

But if this is the revelation that transcends law and human possibility because it is the work of God (Isa. 53:10) in His depth of wisdom and knowledge (Rom. 11:33), it is also true that we must find a relationship with our present-day situation. In our social, economic and political life of today, those who have no standing must find in God's people the recognition of rights and a historical liberation, which is equated with the sacrament of salvation deriving from Him alone. The law and the prophets remain the proof of the fact that God observes, defends, protects, and metes out justice to such people, because the Lord revealed himself in the Exodus from Egypt, above all as liberator (*goel*). It is not God the Creator who is present in the history of mankind, but the Redeemer, who intervenes to liberate those without dignity, and in so doing shows Himself to be master of heaven and earth.

2. ISRAEL, A PEOPLE WITHOUT DIGNITY

According to the Jewish understanding of the first ode of Isaiah the people of Israel are glimpsed as being a people without dignity among nations. It is seen thus from its birth to the present-day, but it is above all true that the Old Testament presents the chosen people as an alienated mass, slave to the Egyptian imperial power. Jews destined to undertake forced labour, under oppressive overlords (*anah*) who treated them harshly (Exod. 1:11 ff.), were compelled to undergo a policy of birth-control or genocide on the part of the Pharaoh (Exod. 1:15 ff.). God bent down towards them and sent Moses to bring about their liberation.

From slavery in Egypt the Jews were called to the service of God. From their low standing they were elevated: 'to be delivered from bondage, to be freedmen and free, to be redeemed, to be God's chosen people, a treasure to all peoples, a kingdom of priests and a holy nation' (Exod. 6:6-7 and 19:5-6).

The Exodus constitutes a radical break with Egypt, a revolutionary event which is to create a new situation for the people of Israel. It means a change of structures, in which it will no longer be possible to return to that slavery to which God's chosen people had been subjected. At this point the law intervenes, in the constantly repeated adage: 'You shall not do as they do in the land of Egypt where you dwelt' (Lev. 18:3). The Exodus does not merely constitute a simple overturning of the relationships between oppressors and oppressed. It is an authoritative foundation for the law which must make Israel not only a land of freedmen but of liberators with respect to all other men. Israel, having experienced what it means to be a people without dignity or standing, from now on has a law which will mean that what it has suffered will not be repeated elsewhere. Consequently a series of legal prescriptions comes into being, with the sole aim of conferring status upon those with none, precisely because Israel herself had none in the land of Egypt (Deut. 10:19 and 24:22 and Exod. 22:20).

The Torah draws attention to the wretched members of society, in a unique legal pronouncement, quite unheard of amongst the surrounding Middle Eastern cultures of the time. It affirms, in a rather Utopian manner, but none the less strongly, that in reality 'there will be no poor among you' (Deut. 15:4-5) in Israel and that 'there shall be one law for the native and for the stranger who sojourns among you' (Exod. 12:49).

From generation to generation there will be the celebration of the real Passovers as the very centre of the law, and it must never become allegorical or spiritualistic. It is a liberating event which has to be personalised and socialised and so will be actively at odds with any attempt to offend the dignity of humankind on the part of rulers and oppressors.

At the Passover each Jew, in the name of Israel, but with a message of hope for all men as its objective, will proclaim in all its historical force that faith in God is to be equated with liberation: 'In every epoch each person is obliged to think of himself as having taken part in the Exodus from Egypt. . . . The Lord leads us from slavery to freedom, from bitterness to joy, from mourning to celebration, from darkness into light, from loss of dignity to dignity . . .' (*Misnha*). From that day of the Exodus, not only Israel[4] but the slave, the immigrant, the oppressed person, the proletariat were restored to the position of free men. All oppression from that day on is transitory, because the seed of liberty, sown at the Exodus, has passed into the world and has never failed.   ˙

3. THE STATUS OF THE IMMIGRANT FOREIGNER

Among those described as poor in the Old Testament, are those people called foreigners or, as it would be better translated today, immigrants.

They live in the land of Israel, or are pilgrims in it. Their situation has become crystallised as one of poverty. They are inferior to those who enjoy all rights of citizenry. The *gher* has no land or familiar surroundings: in the Hebrew mind he was more wretched than the poor man, because the latter was recognised socially, had a place in that society, which was based on blood ties and kinship. The poor man would find solidarity in his surroundings while the foreigner who, often for reasons of famine and hardship in his own country, had come to Israel, risked non-acceptance of his person and non-recognition of his identity. Monarchic Israel therefore elaborates the rights of the immigrant, and this category does indeed seem to be most greatly protected in the Torah.

The foreigner must be loved (Deut. 10:13), he must not be ill-treated or oppressed (Exod. 22:20) nor must he be judged as though he possessed fewer rights than the citizen (Deut. 24:17) but he must be judged under one law only (Exod. 12:48) and with one sentence only (Lev. 24:22).

On stone the law prescribes: 'The stranger who sojourns with you shall be to you as the native among you, and you shall love him as yourself; for you were strangers in the land of Egypt' (Lev. 19:34). We therefore witness the elevation of the foreigner to the status of person, in a series of meticulous enactments which cannot be attested elsewhere in the ancient East. But the law, precisely because the Torah as way implies forward movement, does not remain a cold static thing, but demands at all times up-to-date and fresh interpretation so that the juridical principles therein may always be practically realised. If the foreigner is a fugitive from slavery, he will not be returned to his master, and if he remains poor, he will always be able to share the rights of the poor of Israel, working in the fields and vineyards (Deut. 24:17 ff.). He will take advantage of the labour laws which provide for weekly rest for him too (Deut. 5:12 ff.).

The immigrant also—and let the Torah be compared to the present-day situation of immigrants in the so-called better-off countries!—is not a man forever wrapped up in work: rest is compulsory, so that he is almost 'sentenced' to his vocation for liberty and to *shalom* even in a foreign land. No alienation must be attached to work, not even where the lack of a right to own land in Israel is concerned, since this could lead to the sacrifice of all his energies in an attempt to return to his own land as rich as he can make himself.

The immigrant, therefore, is a man of dignified status, who finds justice in God and who turns to him as to a person who directly protects him by hearing his cry and by being roused to anger (Exod. 22:20-22). If, however, we stopped here, the biblical message concerning this category would be greatly mutilated. In reality, after the Babylonian exile, when Israel was immigrant upon a foreign soil, the prophets identify believers and the pious the (*hassidim*) with the poor (*anawim*) and also with foreigners. This is how Judaism prepared the way for the New Testament where Christians are often called foreigners and pilgrims (Eph. 2:19, 1 Pet. 1:1, 2:11; Heb. 11:3 etc.). Nor should it be forgotten that in the rabbinical tradition the expression taken from Psalm 120:5: 'Woe is me that I sojourn as a stranger', as also the words of Psalm 119:19: 'I am a sojourner on the earth', are those of God himself and not of the psalmist. To the hearer, it is God who becomes the stranger (foreigner) and pilgrim, and who declares his love for him, that he might give full dignity to his children, who see this dignity ill-recognised by men.

4. THE OPPRESSED, THE ORPHAN, THE WIDOW

No poor men should exist on the land which is owned solely by the Lord, and which is divided in possession among the various tribes. Poverty, however, appeared in the person of the exploited (*ani*) and the non-owner (*dal*). This fact never constituted an accusation against God, but against those men who deny solidarity with their neighbours. The Torah, therefore, also intervenes in favour of this category, adducing the very fact that the land was given to those who had been exploited and non-owners in the Egyptian house of slavery. The 'right of the poor' aims to create the solidarity which had been lacking during the sedentary life which was accompanied by transgression of precepts (Deut. 15:4-5).

The vision of poverty as a malediction, as witnessed in the old patriarchal tradition very soon gives way to the vision of poverty created by the rich. From Elias to Zephaniah, their abuse of power, their injustice and the oppression which creates the poor and keeps them in this state, are all denounced. For Jeremiah 'knowledge of God' becomes the judgment of the cause of the poor or the proletariat! (Jer. 22:16). The exploitation of labourers, the non-recognition of their status, the negation of justice which is their due, leads to the invective of the prophets. The latter end by condemning even those religious and liturgical practices which have assumed the guise of self-justification before God. They are hypocrites, stained with the blood of the poor (Isa. 1:14 ff.; Isa. 3:14-15, 5:8 ff., 10:1; Mic. 2:1-2; Amos 2:6 ff.; Jer. 22:13; Hosea 12:8; Zeph. 1:11 etc.).

Those possessing land and estates are radically and definitely condemned in the whole of the teaching of the prophets, while the dignified status of those who possess nothing (*dallat ha harez*) is upheld. They become the faithful 'whose life is holy in the hands of IHWH'.

Among these are the orphan and the widow, who find themselves by chance in a situation of need. This situation can be corrected if they are given the chance of gleaning the corn and other similar activities. On the death of her husband the widow returned his patrimony to the lord, and thus was without means of support. The orphan often fell on hard times as a result of iniquitous processes of succession. In the prophets, however, their rights and their status are of great importance, and God is their vindicator. These weak people constitute the area of activity of the Lord, his assembly of the poor, the poor and humble people of Israel, among whom the Lord God as Saviour, will show Himself (Zeph. 3:12-17). The Church of the Poor is by now the subject of prophecy.

5. THE DIGNITY OF THE SLAVE

In Israel, as in the surrounding world, there were slaves, even though the phenomenon was not so widely attested as in the Ancient Middle East. How was slavery born? Perhaps as a result of war, perhaps through direct purchase (Deut. 20:10-18 and the contradictory 7:1-6; Lev. 25:44 ff.). Some slaves were public property, in the service of the State, while others depended exclusively on private individuals. Slavery may also have originated as payment for a debt (Lev. 25:39). Perhaps, however, to speak of slavery is to be imprecise, at least where the alienation of the person is concerned, where a man, as a man, belongs to another. In reality, we are concerned more with the giving of a service, where one man hires himself out to another, selling the other his work. This at least seems to be the case among the Israelites of the Exodus (Exod. 21:2-3): 'When you buy a Hebrew slave, he shall serve six years, and in the seventh he shall go out free, for nothing.' If, in fact, there was a division of class, between owner and slave, this was accidental, not structural. The code of Hammurabi provides us with an instructive comparison. In this code the slave must be freed after three years (from which one would deduce greater magnanimity on the part of Sumerian legislation), but in reality Hammurabi's code is dealing with rich men who have fallen on bad times and hence into slavery: 'by nature they were free, but by accident, *per accidens*, could become slaves'—thus the right to liberty after three years. In the code, the problem of natural slaves is not posed at all. It was, therefore, the intention of the code, to keep the status quo, to re-establish class divisions just as soon as the system was upset. On the other hand the code of the covenant, in the Torah, demonstrates the opposite intention. This will not permit the slave to become a social class or category but provides for the legal mechanism whereby man's vocation to freedom, including that of the slave, may be approved. It is, for this reason, that the law of compulsory freedom after seven years comes into being. Observation of this law in the history of Israel, seems, however, to be rare, if we except Jeremiah's testimony of the proclamation of the liberty of slaves (Jer. 34:8-10). There is then, in the law, a statute of the slave, which recognises that he is not an object belonging to his master, but a person of dignity with rights which the master is bound to observe until he gives him his liberty. 'In Israel each individual possesses inviolable rights, and it is through the conservation of these that the harmony of society may be guaranteed.'[5]

The case of the Jew who, at the end of the 'sabbatical' year, wished to remain 'slave' to his master, because he so loved him, is indeed significant. In reality, what happened was that the state of slavery ceased and a state of adoption took its place. This was confirmed in a ceremony in which the slave's ear-lobe was pierced. He became a domestic servant, no longer a slave.

The master will willingly bestow freedom upon his slave and will bless him as he lets him go (Deut. 15:18). In the Word of God man's search for freedom and dignity must always be recognised.

It is highly prophetic that when this statute of slaves is not respected, and the Israelites who ought formally to have given slaves their freedom repent, it is not only an ethical law that has been violated but the alliance (*berit*) with God (Jer. 34:10-22).

In defence of slaves, God intervenes and punishes, to the point that, in the hands of Babylon, the king of Judah, his lords and all those who had not given their slaves freedom, became slaves themselves.

6.   WHY WAS DIGNITY GRANTED TO THOSE IN ISRAEL WHO DID NOT POSSESS IT?

In conclusion, we do not wish to give an answer in structural terms, as Marxist or materialistic interpretations of the law of Israel would have it. We wish only to point out that the religious conscience of Israel (the superstructural element) led to a definition of the dignified status of each and every individual, even of those most despised. Whether poor, orphaned, widowed, a foreigner or a slave, God bent down towards those whose status was not one of dignity in order to raise them up and free them. For Judaism this category of person remains, and will remain, a sacrament of historical Israel saved by God. For the believer in Christ, the sacrament of the servant of IHWH is the Messiah who so demeaned Himself that He was the victim of a shameful death in order that justice might be found—justice in the God who raised Him from the dead.

Translated by Lorna M. Gillespie

Notes

1. See J. L. Vesco 'Les Lois sociales du livre de l'alliance' *Revue Thomiste* 68 (1968) 241-265; C. van Leevwen *Le Développement du sens social en Israel avant l'ère chrétienne* (Assen 1955); H. van Oyen *Ethique de l'ancien testament* (Genève 1974); H. W. Wolff *Anthropologie de l'ancien testament* (Genève 1974) pp. 168-179; H. M. Nunez Albacete *Tipos de pobre en el antiguo testamento* (Madrid 1966).

2. See Enzo Bianchi 'Povertà e richezza nella bibbia' *Servitium* 25-26 (1972) 277-309.

3. Such analogies from the 'negative man' of the Frankfurt School and the servant of the Isaiah were described at a seminar of Italian Biblical Scholars by L. Dani, Verona, September 1975.

4. It must be noted that the Passover seder is not a national ceremony and that the Jewish people are not personally at the centre of the Passover. The name of Moses the liberator does not appear in the Haggadad ritual.

5. J. Hour *La Morale de l'alliance* (Paris 1966) p. 78.

Jon Sobrino

Jesus' Relationship with the Poor and Outcasts: Its Importance for Fundamental Moral Theology

1. THE IMPORTANCE OF THE SUBJECT FOR CHRISTIAN MORAL THEOLOGY

THE GOSPEL narratives clearly show Jesus surrounding himself with and favouring sinners, publicans, the sick, lepers, samaritans, pagans and women throughout his life. This overall fact is accepted as a basic characteristic of his praxis.[1] The usual conclusion drawn from it is—correctly—that if even these people were favoured by Jesus—which means that God's love for them is made plain—then all men possess the dignity of sons of God and all men are truly brothers.

This conclusion, however, however important it may be, is not enough to demonstrate the importance of the fact for moral theology. The lessons drawn from it have served, historically, to work out basic principles of Christian anthropology, and to inspire codes of moral practice, such as the traditional duty to help those in need. But understanding of the relationship between Jesus and the poor and outcasts cannot achieve its *systematic* value without setting these actions of his in the context of his fundamental praxis, and without seeing this relationship as fundamental to his praxis.

What has to be done is to ask what is the basic lesson of Christian morality as it appears in the gospels, and to see Jesus' relationship with the poor and outcasts as the basic enactment of his moral praxis rather than as one more aspect of this which, however constant and worthy, still bears only an arbitrary relationship to the essence of his praxis.

The basic moral question can be put in these words: What do we have to do in order to bring about the kingdom of God in history?2 Here we must stress two points: first, we must determine the notion of what is to form the object of a praxis, in this case the kingdom of God; second, we must decide the Christian form of that praxis which will ensure that the kingdom of God comes about. So when we come to analyse the relationship of Jesus to the poor and outcasts, we need to see what this relationship implies for the notion of the kingdom of God, the *bonum morale* to be brought about, and the ethical form praxis must take, that is, the *virtus* that will make this praxis Christian. We then have to see whether what we learn from the relationship is really essential to the very constitution of the notion of the kingdom of God and to the Christian constitution of a praxis able to bring this kingdom into being.

2. THREE INITIAL POINTS

In view of the importance of the poor and outcasts for practical morality, three points are worth making at the outset in order to set Jesus' relationship with them in their historical and existential context.

(i) Today, as in Jesus' time, the poor and outcast make up the majority of the human race. This quantitative fact carries a qualitative charge. If Christianity is characterised by its universal claims, whether made on the basis of creation or of the final consummation, what affects majorities should be a principle governing the degree of authenticity and historical verification of this universalism. A fundamental morality, including one originating in Jesus, should certainly possess a universal direction, but it should be processed through the historical universalism of majorities. Otherwise, the universality it claims will be a euphemism, an irony or a mythified ideologisation. The *'misereor super turbas'* attributed to Jesus (Mark 6:34) should be a foregoing but necessary focus for determining fundamental morality, not only because of the subjective merciful approach it demonstrates, but equally because the object of the mercy is the majority.

(ii) These majorities are not only sum totals of individuals who are poor and outcasts as individuals, but also collectivities made up of social groups. As *groups*, they will require, and there will be required for them, a different code of moral practice from what would be required for purely interpersonal relationships. As *social* groups, moral practice will necessarily result, even if this is not the direct intention, from its setting within the totality of social reality, which is conflictive and antagonistic, and moral practice will therefore have direct repercussions on the whole of society. So the plurals of the gospel stories with their antagonistic character—the poor, sinners, etc., contrasted with the rich, the Pharisees, etc.—will have to be evaluated apart from the scenes in which Jesus related to individuals alone.

(iii) The problem for these majorities is not only, or even primarily, that they are declared to be or treated as those without dignity, those not explicitly recognised as sons of God, or, more precisely, as persons who are subjects with the rights of subjects. Their indignity has an earlier rooting in a social reality, whether on the level of socio-economic infrastructure or that of religious superstructure. In the gospel narratives, these groups of persons are described under the general heading of 'the poor', suffering under the yoke of some form of material oppression, and of 'outcasts' because of their religious affiliations or because they exercise professions held to be conducive to immorality. Jesus' actions were designed not only to declare their dignity in the sight of God, but to mount a radical assault on the causes of their social indignity—the material conditions of their existence and the religious concepts of their time. The importance of this observation for basic ethics lies in showing that mere declarations of the dignity before God of the lowest are insufficient unless they lead to an unmasking and transforming of the roots of their lowliness.

3. THE KINGDOM OF GOD IS FOR THE POOR AND OUTCASTS

If a morality stemming from Jesus concerns itself with bringing about the kingdom of God, it is obviously important at the outset to decide what constitutes this. Yet Jesus himself, who is described as using the term 'kingdom of God' so often, did not precisely describe what he meant by it.[3] He declares that the kingdom is coming and that it is 'good news' (Mark 1:15; Matt. 4:23; Luke 4:43). It might be possible to try to analyse the various concepts of the kingdom of God prevalent at the time and to decide which of them, or what synthesis of them, might have influenced Jesus' proclamation of it, but this would not seem a very fruitful approach. The statement that 'the specific content of the kingdom stems from his ministry and actions, viewed as a whole'[4] seems to offer a better approach. This is how his relations with the poor and outcasts take on such fundamental importance.

(i) Jesus announced the kingdom as good news to the poor (Luke 4:18; cf. 7:22; Matt. 11:5) and declared that it was made up of the poor (Luke 6:20; cf. Matt. 5:3). This establishes a basic correlation between the good news and its principal (or only[5]) recipients, and indirectly shows what this good news consists of. If this kingdom is for the poor, if salvation comes not to the just but to sinners, if publicans and prostitutes will enter the kingdom before the pious, then the very situation of those for whom the kingdom is destined must demonstrate—though initially *sub specie contrarii*—the central content of the good news. In that case, the kingdom of God must be not a universal symbol of Utopian hope, interchangeable with any other Utopia, but more specifically the hope of those groups who suffer under some kind of material and social oppression.[6] The good news must then be, firstly and directly, what today is called liberation, whose biblical antecedents are to be found more in the line of the prophets than in the apocalyptic view of universal history.

Before prematurely spiritualising the poor and universalistically extrapolating the notion of the kingdom, it is as well to remember that those for whom the kingdom is destined are those who are most deprived of life at its most basic levels. In the passage where Jesus replies to the envoys from John the Baptist, the poor are described as the blind, the lame, the deaf, and so on. J. Jeremias interprets this passage not in any spiritualised sense, but as meaning a reference to 'the situation of such people, which in the thought of the time could no longer be called life'.[7] The good news is then the bringing of life to those who have been denied it and deprived of it in the secular sphere.

The kingdom of God, that which is to be built, is therefore in correlation with those who are most deprived of life. So to gain a working idea of the content of the kingdom of God we must adopt the viewpoint of those who lack life, power and dignity, and not pretend that there can be another and better viewpoint than theirs. In this way the idea of the kingdom will not be paralysed by the abstract universalism of its content nor by a precipitate imposition of the eschatological reserve on it.[8] The poor, sinners and the despised are the necessary, though not absolutely sufficient,[9] starting-point for an understanding of what is meant by the good news of the kingdom. The ultimate theo-logical reason for this is simply that God loves them and protects them and wishes them to have life.[10]

(ii) Besides this correlation between the kingdom of God and the poor, what the kingdom of God consists of can be discovered by considering Jesus' actions as actions in the service of the kingdom. His specific behaviour toward the poor and outcasts gives no gnostic revelation of what the kingdom is, but does reveal how the kingdom operates in practice. When his actions are praxis—i.e., designed to operate on his surrounding historical circumstances in order to change them in a specific direction—he indirectly but nonetheless effectively shows what the kingdom of God is about. There is therefore a correlation between Jesus' historical service and what the kingdom is to be, provided this service is understood as being for and from the poor and outcasts. Jesus' actions in this respect operates on various levels, which can only briefly be touched on here.

First, there is the action of his words. The positive announcement of the good news is partly in the nature of a proclamation, in that it is an expression of the revelation of the gratuitous mystery of God and— unlike the proclamation of John the Baptist, for instance—of the supremacy of God's love over his judgment and of the partiality of this love. But it is also in the nature of praxis in that it is conducive to the formation of a historical consciousness in the poor and outcasts and in that it is also in fact a vehicle for ideological struggle through its polemical proclamation of the partiality of God.

In this way his words are a proclamation in which the mystery of God is expressed, and also a praxis operating on surrounding historical reality.

With the positive announcement goes the practice of denunciation. The various anathemas condemn not only sinful conduct in itself, but also the behaviour of one social group toward another. Sin is condemned in the name of the good news not only as personal failure of the person in his relationship with God, but also as something preventing the kingdom of God becoming a reality for the poor. The rich are told that their riches are an injustice, that they are the oppressors of the poor (Luke 16:9; 19. 1 ff.); the Pharisees that they do not practice justice and are blind leading the blind (Luke 11:42; Matt. 23:16, 24); the lawyers that they load intolerable burdens on men, burdens that they do not move a finger to lift, that they have taken away the key of knowledge, preventing others going in who wanted to (Luke 11:46, 52; Mark 12:38 ff.); the priests that they have turned the temple into a robbers' den (Mark 11:55 ff.); rulers that they lord it over their people (Mark 10:42).

The typical structure of his indictments and anathemas consists in condemning not only what is intrinsically sinful in the conduct of these social groups, but also the added hypocrisy that such behaviour can be justified in the name of religion. Sinfulness has to have an object: these people are oppressors of the poor. So Jesus' condemnations are at the same time a defence of the poor; they also have a social implication since they are directed against one group and in favour of another, condemning established relationships and thereby working on them. This is the practice of proclamation from the reverse of its negation.

Alongside the action of words in proclamation and denunciation, the gospels show particular actions, which can be summed up in the words 'He has done all things well' (Mark 7:37) and are at their most characteristic in his healings and dealings with sinners. They are normally described as happening in particular situations and addressed to individuals, but the type of person to whom they are addressed and their content, shed light on the meaning of the kingdom.

If Jesus refused to perform miracles for his own justification, if the miracles are never described for the sake of their 'miraculousness', but as works (*erga*), acts of power (*dunameis*), Signs (*semeia*), then they can only be acts that demonstrate the sovereignty of God, that is the kingdom of God (Luke 11:20) over those who are subjected to the sovereignty of evil. The same should be said for the forgiveness of sins. Even if the two scenes in which forgiveness is explicitly described (Mark 2:5; Luke 7:48) cannot be claimed to be historically accurate, what cannot be doubted is that Jesus showed his solidarity with sinners, sitting at table with them (Mark 2:15-17; Luke 7:36-50), in order to show them God's love and so rescue them from their social isolation.

Jesus' specific actions in the service of the kingdom of God show, then, that this is the liberation of the poor and outcasts, and that this liberation should not only be proclaimed as the will of God for the world, but that it should come about in history, that it should be brought to fruition.[11]

4. VOLUNTARY SOLIDARITY WITH THE POOR AND OUTCASTS AS THE WAY TO BRING THE KINGDOM OF GOD INTO BEING

Jesus' relations with the poor and outcasts shows what the kingdom should be in action, but it also shows how it is to be brought about. The means to this can be summed up as voluntary solidarity with the poor and outcasts.

That this should be so does not stem from any *a priori* rationalisation, but follows the logic of the Old Testament witness of the Servant of Yahweh and the historical structure of Jesus' life on earth. The kingdom of God is announced and brought to the poor in a contrary and antagonistic world of sin. The good news is good not primarily because it adds to and goes beyond the positive element in a given situation, but because it goes against it. What the theology of the servant affirms is that fulness passes through the moment of taking on denial and cannot be achieved from the inertia of the merely positive. While in the first song the servant is given the mission of spreading law and justice on earth (Isa. 42:1-9), in the fourth he is burdened with the sin of the world so that this fulness can be brought to fruition (Isa. 52:13-53).[12]

This is the basic structure of Jesus' activity, as he in fact carried it out, independently of his possible view of himself as the servant and of his first vision of how his mission was to be accomplished. Effective defence of the poor involves removing the real, objective sin that impoverishes them; this sin cannot be eradicated without taking on the condition of the poor; their dignity cannot be given back to them without taking on their indignity.

This process is well illustrated on the theoretical level in the scene of the temptations, which should not be taken as one specific incident, and certainly not as happening at the outset of his ministry, but as an illustration of the climate and environment in which his life unfolded. They demonstrate his objective choice of service in the manner of the servant, without the power that—even used in the service of the powerless— would have removed him from the reality and consequence of poverty, indignity and persecution.

Jesus, in the specific historical reality of his life, conceived his mission in such a way that it had to follow a historical course leading inevitably to his being deprived of security, dignity and life itself—the historical course of voluntary impoverishment. While it is difficult to point to particular incidents in the narratives that illustrate this process in action, the whole tenor of the gospels shows it at work, and his death on the cross proves it. Jesus was stripped of his dignity, as is shown by the insults hurled at him and in the theologised scenes in which his adversaries seek to throw him out of the synagogue and the temple, a real excommunication. He was stripped of security, as appears from the form of persecution mounted against him shortly before his death, which the gospels put back to the early part of his ministry (Mark 3:6; Luke 4:28-30) in order to stress the atmosphere of persecution in which he operated. Finally, Jesus was deprived of his own life, the true and final impoverishment.

What needs to be stressed in this objective process of impoverishment is that Jesus undertook it out of solidarity with the poor. The persecution he underwent can be understood in a personalist sense in view of the attacks he made on various social groups, but it will not be understood in depth without appreciating the element of defence of the poor contained in these attacks. The famous five controversies in Mark 2:1-3, 5 are based on a defence of the sick, sinners and the hungry. When he unmasked the hypocrisy of the Pharisees it was to show them avoiding duty to parents in need (Mark 7:1-13).[12] His impoverishment stems from something much deeper than asceticism, from a voluntary solidarity with the poor and outcasts.

The requirements he laid on others also show that same movement in the direction of basic impoverishment: the call to follow him in order to carry out a mission in poverty, to leave home and family, to take up the cross; these are not arbitrary requirements that he could equally not have imposed. They are requirements in the direct line of impoverishment. The beatitudes show the same approach from a different angle: the poor in material things are called to appreciate their poverty and live it as poverty in the spirit, thereby participating actively in the movement of impoverishment.[13]

This active process of impoverishment which Jesus practised in his life is simply the historical version of what was later theologised as his transcendent impoverishment: the incarnation and *kenosis*. Note that this transcendent impoverishment took historical form not only through the assumption of human flesh, but also through the assumption of solidarity with the poor and outcasts.

5. FUNDAMENTAL MORALITY AND THEO-LOGY

The actual relations between Jesus and the poor and outcasts show the *bonum*, the bonum of fundamental Christian morality to lie in bringing the kingdom of God into being for the poor, and the basic *way* in which this is to be brought about is voluntary impoverishment in solidarity with the poor. We need to ask at this stage whether these observations, though obviously important in the gospels, are really of basic importance, greater than any others, for Christian morality. To determine this we need to ask the further question, I think, of whether this interpretation of the kingdom gives the best idea of the ultimate reality of the God in whom Jesus believed and in whom Christians believe.

This interpretation involves both revelation of God and the approach to God through a faith that is specifically Christian. Unlike a basically *gnostic* conception it is not a matter of merely knowing *about* God, but of knowing his will and how this is put into effect. Hence the importance of approaching God through his mediation of the kingdom of God that we have to bring about. Unlike a directly *universalist* conception, it stresses the constitutive partiality of God toward those who have historically been most deprived of love, right and justice. Unlike a purely *natural* conception of God, it lays emphasis on the scandalous element in God's own reality, what we call the *kenosis*, the impoverishment and humiliation of the son.

Such a *Christianised* conception of God should be the ultimate basis for moral theology. Inversely, only the historical embodiment of this type of basic moral theology can provide an idea, beyond generic statements, of what God is really like.[14] The generically accepted correlation between God and the poor and outcasts becomes both rewarding and challenging when seen from the standpoint of Jesus' actual dealings with them, and when this relationship becomes the principle for both positing and resolving the basic question of morality.

Translated by Paul Burns

Notes

1. This study does not set out to be an exegesis of the various synoptic traditions and their contributions to the subject. I am not trying to discover what in their accounts of Jesus is genuinely historical as opposed to historicised in the early communities, but I am assuming that there exists a sufficient deposit of historicity related to the subject to enable the data to be ordered systematically.

2. See I. Ellacuría 'La iglesia de los pobres, sacramento histórico de la liberación' *ECA* (Oct.-Nov. 1977) 710 ff.

3. See W. Kasper *Jesús, el Cristo* (Salamanca 1976) p. 86; E. Schillebeeckx *Jesus. An Experiment in Christology* (New York 1979) p. 143.

4. E. Schillebeeckx *Jesus*; J. Sobrino 'Jesús y el reino de Dios' *Sal Terrae* (May 1978) 350.

5. See J. Jeremias *Teología del nuevo testamento* (Salamanca 1974) I p. 142.

6. On this duality of meaning in the concept of the poor, see *ibid*. pp. 134-138.

7. *Teología* p. 128.

8. This does not mean reducing the kingdom of God to the basic levels of life, but it means they should be borne in mind in order not to forget its basic requirement when speaking of more abundant life and eschatological fulness in accordance with the gospel.

9. The mere fact of poverty is important in determining the nature of the kingdom of God, but not all poverty is automatically efficacious for historical salvation. See I. Ellacuría 'Las bienaventuranzas como carta fundacional de la iglesia de los pobres' in *Iglesia de los pobres y organizaciones populares* ed. Various (San Salvador 1979) 118.

10. As the *Puebla Document* recognised in n. 1142: 'For this reason alone, the poor deserve preferential treatment, whatever their moral or personal situation. . . . God takes their part and loves them'. See G. Gutiérrez 'Pobres y liberacíon en Puebla' *Páginas* (Apr. 1979) 11 ff.

11. See C. E. Freire *Devolver el evangelio a los pobres* (Salamanca 1978) pp. 269 ff.

12. See P. Benoit and M.-E. Boismard *Sinopsis de los cuatro evangelios* (Bilbao 1976) pp. 96-110, 215-217.

13. See I. Ellacuría article cited in note 1.

14. Otherwise such statements remain paradoxical and without practical effect. One might ask what real results these fine words by Karl Barth have had, written forty years ago and quoted by Gutiérrez in the article cited in note 10 at p. 1: 'God places himself always unconditionally and passionately on this side, and only on this side: always against the proud, always in favour of the humble, always against those who have rights and privileges, always in favour of those who are denied and deprived of their rights' (*Kirchliche Dogmatik* [¹Zurich 1940] I p. 434).

Jost Eckert

The Realisation of Fellowship in the Earliest Christian Communities

OUR image of the first Christian communities is largely determined by Luke's *Acts of the Apostles* and the letters of St Paul. This goes primarily for the original Jewish-Christian community of Jerusalem, the mixed Jewish and Gentile members of the community of Antioch in Syria, and the probably most important of St Paul's foundations, the community of Corinth. Any such construction must not, however, overlook the fact that there are gaps in the information provided in *Acts*, that Luke occasionally allowed himself to idealise a little (see 2:42-47) and that Paul's letters give us only a limited view of the actual life of the community. Here one might point out that, unless there had been abuses in the celebration of the Eucharist in Corinth, abuses which he had to deal with, we would not have a clue about the celebration of the Eucharist in Corinth.

Other communities, mentioned in the New Testament, provide us with a picture which varies a great deal in clarity. It is therefore precisely there that we have difficulty in understanding exactly how these communities lived. Inter-Christian relationships developed according to the life and teaching of Jesus, and so the tradition and further development of the evangelical message were influenced by the way actual community problems were tackled.

1. THE NEW OUTLOOK ON LIFE OF THE JESUS MOVEMENT

The history of Christendom did not start with the local communities but with Jesus Christ, the wandering messenger of God's kingdom, and the gathering movement which, launched by him and inspired by the Easter event, set out on its way to this kingdom.

The mentality of the earliest Christians did not spring from their desire to found a new religion which would make its presence felt in this world for a long time as an institution endowed with a growing bureaucracy and building a lot of churches. They rather saw themselves as an eschatological movement which expected final salvation to come, not from the traditional Jewish faith nor from secular reforms in this world, but from the Christ who would come again in power and glory (see 1 Thess. 1:9 f.; 1 Cor. 7:29-31, 16:22; Mark 13).

Jesus' words to those who wanted to follow him, with their radical exhortation to leave everything and to let go even of the customary ties for the sake of the kingdom (see Luke 9:59 f., 9:61 f., 14:26), remained eschatological pointers, particularly actual, though somewhat diluted (see 1 Cor. 9:5), for the original leaders, the apostles, prophets and other missionaries who, like Jesus, had no fixed abode but spread the gospel as roving missionaries.[1]

Yet this following of Jesus did not lead the disciples to a flight from the world into a communal ghetto as a separatist and élitist group, as was the case of Qumran; Jesus' openness to all mankind, particularly to those who were religiously and socially despised, remained a basic characteristic of the Jesus movement. The stories about exorcism in the gospels and Acts show that those possessed by the devil were accepted and socially integrated in the Christian community where from the beginning members of the various religious and social groups of Jewry clearly found a new sense of belonging.[2] This was made possible through the new concept of man which Jesus brought. For him, indeed, man was not to be judged by his origin or by his present moral and religious qualities but by his willingness to look for his future to the salvation implied in God's kingdom. It obviously required a protracted historical development before the consequences of this eschatological view of salvation were finally accepted with regard to the gentiles.

The 'Utopian' ethic of the Sermon on the Mount (Matt. 5:7) sharpened the moral commandments of the Torah but softened the cultural and religious ones. It did not intend to lead to an anxiety-dominated separatism based on an inhuman tyrannical law but rather to a new radical sense of fellowship based on the awareness that believers, too, can live only on the assumption that there is forgiveness (Luke 11:4; Matt. 6:12).[3] This new fellowship goes beyond this in that it is motivated by the belief in a Jesus who identified with the least of the brethren (Matt. 25:40) and who died for the sinners (Mark 10:45, 14:24; 1 Cor. 15:3).

2. THE EARLIEST COMMUNITY: THAT OF JERUSALEM

The way in which Acts tells us about the life of this primitive community (2:42-47, 4:32-35)[4] was clearly meant to convey an ideal picture of the Church at its origin. Luke simplified the story (see the idea of the twelve apostles) and either no longer knew or did not want to know about various problems which existed within the Church (see the way Luke has taken the heat out of the controversy around Paul's theology).[5] This has to be taken into account when we interpret the picture presented by Luke. He may also well have used many traditional reports, and in any case the early days of a community are usually a period of idealism.

With an eye to the Church of his own time Luke stressed that life in the primitive community was marked by the members' faithfulness to 'the teaching of the apostles' and by their 'union' in the faith (2:42a, 4:32). The factors that built up the fellowship were the union of the faithful 'in the breaking of the bread and in prayer' (2:42b) and the celebration of the supper in each other's houses in the joyful expectation of the Lord's coming (2:46). There is no need to deny a core of actual historical truth in his version of the community of goods in the community (2:44 f., 4:32, 34-37), even when one takes account of Luke's concern for the poor and the possible influence of some political philosophy in the text. The need of a fellow Christian could not be ignored by those that were well-to-do, particularly since, according to Jesus' message, wealth contained an inherent threat to the spirit (Mark 10:25). All the same, there was no general renunciation of goods nor any enforced surrender of private property as in Qumran (5:4). The fact that the members still belonged to the Jewish social and religious society (2:46 f., 5:12) saved the community for the time being from numerous problems which would have to be sorted out later with the integration of the gentiles. Within the community and its fellowship the old social and religious forms of discrimination had been overcome. But even Luke could not deny that some differences existed among groups. He simply had to mention the 'Hellenist' members of the Jerusalem community because when, in his historical narrative, he referred to the spread of the gospel 'throughout Judaea and Samaria, and indeed to the ends of the earth' (Acts 1:8), he simply could not by-pass these Greek-speaking Jewish Christians.

Luke links the creation of a group of seven men, under Stephen's leadership, with the complaint of the 'Hellenists' that their widows were overlooked in the daily distribution of aid (Acts 6:1-6). But the way the story is told here is far from clear. Even the Acts cannot maintain that the seven were simply set apart by the twelve apostles for the daily distribution of aid in order to set the apostles free for the proclamation of the gospel. Stephen and Philip are described as evangelists full of the Holy Spirit (6:8-8, 40). It would rather appear that the seven were the leading representatives of the Hellenist Jewish Christians in Jerusalem, and that the widows were neglected not because the twelve were overworked but because there were tensions within the community. Where did these tensions come from?

Then there are the very brief reports on the persecution of the Jerusalem community 'except the apostles' (8:1), Stephen's prophetic criticism of temple and cult (7:46 f.) and his being stoned to death (7:54-60). This shows that the Hellenistic Jewish Christians who came from the diaspora—and were no doubt also motivated by their new faith[6]—had a more liberal approach to the Torah and the religious tradition than the Palestinian Jewish Christians who, at that time, certainly came from the countryside of Galilee. It looks as if only the Hellenists were persecuted. The sociological differences in origin and culture, which were reflected in legal discrimination, clearly created a strain on the Jerusalem community. Yet, the relations between the Hellenists who had been driven out and the original community show that all were concerned to maintain unity and fellowship.

3. THE COMMUNITY OF ANTIOCH

Next in importance after Jerusalem is the community of Antioch in Syria. According to Acts 11:19-26 the expelled Hellenists went there to preach the gospel to the pagans. It seems that this community, composed of Jewish and gentile Christians, provided Paul with the springboard for his mission to the gentiles (Acts 13:1-3, 15:36-40; Gal. 2:11-14).

No doubt there had occasionally been gentiles who were converted, and Luke attaches great importance to the conversion of the pagan centurion Cornelius (10:1-11, 18). But it is difficult to overestimate the consequences of a new development in the history of theology and of the church, and this is that in the community of Antioch the fundamentally equal relationship between the Jewish Christians, united with Abraham through the circumcision, and the uncircumcised gentile Christians became accepted. It is significant that the followers of Jesus were first called 'Christians' in Antioch (Acts 11:26). Christianity clearly began to be dissociated from Judaism. The Jewish-Christian protest against this development[7] and the debate within the Church on this point at the meeting of the apostles round about 50 A.D. show that the historical 'ecumenical' events ran ahead of theology. But the mission to the pagans, which had come about through the expulsion of the Hellenists and which these missionaries took as fully justified in the spirit of Christ, had to be theologically accepted in the Church as a whole. And here the historical *fait accompli* of the mission to the pagans and its success led to theological recognition (see Gal. 2:7-9; Acts 15:12).

However, how little this solved all the problems is made evident by the conflict among the apostles in Antioch which followed the apostolic council in Jerusalem (Gal. 2:11-14).[8] Because of pressure by the faction of James, Kephas, Barnabas and the rest of the Jewish Christians gave up taking part in the Eucharist with the gentile Christians. That it was in fact the Eucharist seems likely. For the time being at least they abandoned their liberal and Christian practice and yielded to the conservative Jewish Christian principle which required the Jewish Christians to maintain the precepts of the law and, with this, the prohibition to eat with the pagans. In this they based themselves on the conclusion reached at the apostolic council: 'We (Paul and Barnabas) were to go to the pagans and they (Peter and the other Jewish missionaries) to the circumcised' (Gal. 2:9). In criticising this decision Paul did not mince his words. Whether he had any success in Antioch where he made only a brief stay is doubtful since he never refers to it in his dispute with his Judaistic opponents in Galatians and makes no reference to the community of Antioch in any of his other letters. The so-called apostolic decree (Acts 15:19 f., 28 f.), which Paul does not know (just as, on the other hand, Acts does not know about the conflict at Antioch), probably reflects a theological compromise with which this problem of the community was met at a later date.

It was, however, through the Hellenistic missionaries and communities that a basic principle became established in the Church's practice which Paul expressed in Gal. 3:28: 'There are no more distinctions between Jew and Greek, slave and free, male and female, but all of you are one in Christ Jesus' (see I Cor. 12:13; Col. 3:11). Paul is here speaking in the context of Christian baptism. His dictum therefore means that the new unity in Christ, which believers have achieved in faith and baptism, must be strong enough to overcome the divisiveness of religious, social and sexual differences. This basic law of Christianity had a powerful appeal but was not easy to put into practice, as Paul's first letter to the Corinthians shows only too clearly.

4. THE COMMUNITY OF CORINTH

Of all the communities which Paul scattered around in the West the largest and most lively one was, not Athens, chained to its traditions, but Corinth. A new town founded about 44 B.C., it became the place of exchange for money and mind between East and West, and, in the process, the melting-pot of humanity, of whatever ethnic, social or religious colour.

It is true that at the beginning the success of this community in gaining new members was powerfully influenced by Paul's personality and by his insight into the new message of salvation, since it met a widespread need for liberation.[9] Yet, it is clear that very early on the experience of fellowship at the meetings and of coping with practical problems appealed to many, particularly the socially underprivileged. According to 1 Cor. 1:26 the community did not contain many that were 'wise in the ordinary sense of the word', nor 'influential', nor 'belonging to the noble families'; most of them were 'little people'. But the community problems discussed in 1 Cor. show also that people with property, culture and social prestige were not exactly lacking.[10] On this point one really should not underrate the 'house' communities (see Acts 18:7 f.; 1 Cor. 1:16, 16:15) which were religiously motivated (see 1 Cor. 16:19, 1:3, 2:46, 12:12, 20, 20:8, 20). Such communities were common in the cultural communities of Hellenism as well as at the beginnings of the synagogue in the diaspora.[11] All this was 'community-building'. At the same time they were a fruitful environment for missionary work. No doubt, they could also lead to creation of groups.

Another noteworthy feature was the large measure of freedom, equality and fellowship which led to a charismatic community where everyone's spiritual experiences were highly treasured (1 Cor. 2:12-14). Everybody could speak at their meetings, and nobody objected to a woman speaking up when moved by the Spirit (11:5). During his stay of about 18 months (Acts 18:11) Paul clearly did not aim at setting up a hierarchical structure based on a distribution of official functions.

This high appreciation of the gifts of the Spirit (1 Cor. 12:1) nevertheless led to an overestimation of such extraordinary manifestation of the Spirit as glossolalia. The result was a split in the community between the charismatics, i.e., those noticeably endowed with the Spirit, and those who felt they were lacking in something and got worried. To the charismatics or 'spirituals' belonged those who were convinced they were equipped with 'wisdom' or 'knowledge' (gnosis) (8:1, 12:8, 14:1-4) and they probably included a large number of the well-to-do and the better educated. Among these rather confident charismatics (4:8, 19 f.) Christian freedom led to the assertion that 'for me there are no forbidden things' (6:12, 10:23), and from there to a moral libertinism (6:12-20) and the eating of food sacrificed to the idols (8:4, 10). Some even took part in the sacrificial meal in some temple (8:10), though most of them limited themselves to doing this when there was some social function they had to go to or to buying such meat in the market. The 'weaker' brethren were shocked by this behaviour of the 'strong' ones (8:7-15).[12] Paul approached this issue by pointing out that the gifts of the Spirit covered a whole range of charismata (12:4-11) which are all complementary like the members of the body and should be exercised according to the requirements of the community which has to be built up (12:7, 14). Since 'everybody has his own particular gifts from God' (7:7) and love is the one 'that is better than any of them' (13; Gal. 5:22), every Christian is fundamentally a 'charismatic' (Gal. 5:13-6, 10). In the fellowship of the Christian community there is no room for clericalism. With regard to the eating of food sacrificed to idols Paul maintains the principle underlying the free, enlightened Christian position 'that idols do not really exist in the world' (8:4) but Christian witness should be borne when required (10:20 f., 28 f.), and Christian freedom should not prove a pitfall for the brother (8:9, 13). In spite of his conviction that sexual and social differences have been overcome in Christ, Paul had no intention of altering the normal ways by which this world proceeds since 'the world as we know it is passing away' (7:31). Women are advised to accept the conventions (11:13-16) and slaves are told to accept the facts of their situation (7:20). Yet, he gives women equal rights with man (7:3-5, 10-17) and the slave becomes the Lord's freedman[13] while the freeman becomes the 'slave of Christ' (7:22).

What upset Paul profoundly after he had left Corinth was that parties arose there based on a kind of personality cult, which might lead to communities based on a conflict of personalities (1:12), and by the same token would give the lie to the unity in Christ (1:13, 3:11). He also condemned the kind of divisiveness which came to the fore at the celebration of the Eucharist (11:17-34).[14]

Several members of the community, probably the more well-to-do, who could arrive earlier than the slaves and the poor who had to finish their job first, brought along their own food and took it before the service started so that at the beginning of the actual celebration of the Eucharist 'one person goes hungry while another is getting drunk' (11:21). This threatened to become a purely 'sacramental' occasion without any genuine contribution to the building of the community. For Paul this 'is no longer the Lord's Supper' (11:20). When the celebration of the Eucharist, which should proclaim the death of the Lord and offer the chalice of the new covenant (11:25 f.), showed no growth of Christian fellowship, this whole ritual celebration was misunderstood and became an ineffectual purely sacramental procedure (see also Matt. 5:23 f.). The real significance of the Eucharist is this: 'The bread we break is a communion with the body of Christ. The fact that there is only one loaf means that, though there are many of us, we form a single body, because we all have a share in this one loaf' (1 Cor. 10:17). It is Christianity's enduring mission to bring about this unity.

The tragedy of the history of Christianity is that, after it had achieved the integration of people, all coming from an extremely varied religious, ethnic and social backgrounds, into a single communal fellowship, this unity was time and again broken up by dogmatic differences within the

Church. It was Jesus' declared intention that the will to achieve fellowship should overcome the pharisaic trend towards separatism. Every community of the Christian faith constantly has to re-discover the unifying function of the Lord's supper. 'He who is not with me is against me, and he who does not gather with me scatters' (Matt. 12:30).

Translated by Theo L. Westow

Notes

1. See G. Theissen *Soziologie der Jesusbewegung. Ein Beitrag zur Entstehungsgeschichte des Urchristentums* (Munich 1977).
2. Take, for example, the publican (Mark 2:14) and the zealot (Luke 6:15) who move in Jesus' company.
3. See J. Eckert 'Wesen und Funktion der Radikalismen in der Botschaft Jesu' in *Münchener Theologische Zeitschrift* 24 (1973) 301-325.
4. See also Acts 1:14, 5:12-16, 6:7, 9:31.
5. See J. Eckert 'Paulus und die Jerusalemer Autoritäten nach dem Galaterbrief und der Apostelgeschichte' in *Schriftauslegung. Beiträge zur Hermeneutik des NT und im NT* ed. J. Ernst (Paderborn 1972) pp. 281-311.
6. In his 'Zwischen Jesus und Paulus. Die "Hellenisten", die "Sieben" and Stephanus' *ZThK* 72 (1975) 185, M. Hengel maintains that 'the Jews who came back to Jerusalem from the diaspora . . . were as a rule precisely not "liberal"'. But one should distinguish between the spiritual and religious fluidity of the 'Christian' Jews from the diaspora and the attitude of the other members of the Hellenistic synagogues in Jerusalem.
7. See Acts 11:3, 15:1 f.; Matt. 10:5 f.
8. See the ref. in note 5 and F. Muszner *Der Galaterbrief* (Freiburg 1974) pp. 132-167.
9. See A. Schreiber *Die Gemeinde in Korinth. Versuch einer gruppendynamischen Betrachtung der Entwicklung der Gemeinde von Korinth auf der Basis des ersten Korintherbriefes* (Münster 1977).
10. See G. Theissen 'Soziale Schichtung in der Korinthischen Gemeinde' *ZNW* (1974) 232-272.
11. F. Stuhlmacher 'Urchristliche Hausgemeinden: Der Brief an Philemon' *EKK* (1975) 70-75.
12. See G. Theissen 'Die Starken und Schwachen in Korinth. Soziologische Analyse eines theologischen Streites' *Evang. Theol.* 35 (1975) 155-172.
13. See Philem. 15 f.
14. See G. Theissen 'Soziale Integration und sakramentales Handeln. Eine Analyse von 1 Cor. 11:17-34' *Nov. Test.* 16 (1974) 179-206.

Part II

Some Historical Examples of the Christian Attitude towards the Worthless

Charles Pietri

Christians and Slaves in
the Early Days of
the Church (2nd-3rd Centuries)

'THERE is neither slave nor free . . . for you are all one in Christ Jesus.'
To the throngs of slaves which covered the Roman Empire, fettered
proletarians often tied to the most menial labours and always marked by
the stigma of legal inequality, what message of hope could the apostle's
words bring? The variety of responses, and their theological implications,
is easy to imagine. In the nineteenth century the social Catholics, the
abolitionists, fighting colonial slavery, badly wanted the Church to have
broken the chains of servitude because they were looking for a model for
their protest. But on this point the talent of Moeller, of Ozanam, the
erudite treatises composed by H. Wallon or, at the end of the century, by
P. Allard, could offer little resistance to the assaults of scientific phil-
ology. A protestant theologian, Overbeck (d. 1905)showed that such an
argument could not be based on giving equal weight to the testimonies of
the earliest Church (second-third centuries) and to those of a hagiographic literature forged three centuries later. The success of this critique
gave new force to the whole movement of ideas which, since the
Enlightenment, had only too readily placed the Church on the side of
intolerance and tyranny. If the condition of the slaves improved in antiquity, the credit belongs to Seneca—and to the Stoics, whose influence
on Roman law is stressed even today by legal historians: in social questions Christians do not come off very well when they borrow pagan
philosophers' clothes. But how can the history of slavery be limited to that
of a legislative reform which neglects the pressures of economic mechanisms and the tension of social hatreds? In 1899 the Italian Ciccotti drew

31

on Marx, on Engels, and on the American Cairnes, who had demonstrated the poor profitability of servile labour in the Confederate plantations. The slave system gradually fell apart, provisionally, when it seemed more profitable, more convenient and less dangerous to use free workers. Christian preaching and that of the philosophers was an accompaniment to an evolution which it did little to promote, and—so some writers tell us—these ideologies even checked the movement by calming the revolt of the still fettered slave with the illusory promise of inner freedom. Finally the disappointed apologists turned their guns round; since the early Church could not give them a model for the struggles of the present, it must have committed a sort of sin, a historically irremediable fault.

In this debate, studded with ideological traps which he cannot totally avoid, the historian must arm himself with precautions. First, he must recognise that the Church—this institutional and social fact he is studying—generally combines in the movement of its long history the poor man of Assisi and Torquemada; he cannot exaggerate the importance of the second to the detriment of the first. And for this ancient period is it right to talk of the Church as a powerful, homogeneous force, capable of dominating the State and facing coherently the problems of a slave society? The little communities into which Christianity was fragmented more or less all professed the same faith, but during the early centuries these minorities, submerged in a society which first ignored them and then watched and harrassed them, attempted to solve the problems of their presence in the world so as to achieve the best solution of the problems presented to each by its social composition. Here we must bear in mind the Christians who had come from the synagogue, there a larger group of slaves. And then, to obtain a picture of the society of their time the Christians used a set of mental tools, a whole complex of collective representations in which slavery, like war, was accepted as inevitable. Now the idea of revolution generally suggests the overthrow of a political class or political institutions, a change of structures simply in the sense that the reversal of roles plunges the former masters into servitude. How are we to harmonise Paul's proclamation with the constraints of social life? The initial experiments of the stable communities of the first centuries—before the establishment of a Christian empire in the fourth century—may illustrate the effort the churches made to go beyond declarations of principle, not to produce social teaching, but at least to establish a practice.

1. A CHALLENGE IN PRINCIPLE

At the beginning there is Paul, whose challenge in principle denies slavery all legitimacy. But, for a better understanding of the apostle and of the message of Christian preaching after him, let us not forget Seneca, the first to proclaim so loudly in the Latin West the brotherhood of man and the humanity of slaves. The lawyers repeated after the philosopher that, as far as the natural law was concerned, all men are equal. This equality does not exclude differences, but the real hierarchy does not follow legal conditions. By triumphing over the passions which enslave him, the slave can reach true freedom and surpass his master, who is chained to his desires. But the golden age of natural brotherhood has degenerated into a society in which slavery appears inevitable: the slave must seek an inner freedom by mastering his impatience; the master must treat his servant like a humble friend. To the master Seneca adds a counsel of prudence with this terrible barb: 'Every slave is an enemy.'

The Christians do not speak quite the same language. It is not the law of nature which makes men equal, but the law of God. The apologist Minucius Felix explained this in the first years of the third century to the pagan intelligentsia: 'We call each other "brother" as men who have one and the same God as father. . . .' For the rest, as all Christian writing after Paul repeats—Irenaeus of Lyons, the apologists—there is no hierarchy; before Christ redeemed us, all mankind lived in slavery to sin. There is no need to stress here a well-known development of Pauline theology, except to note that, in looking for an analogy, the apostle spontaneously assimilates slavery to evil and sin. This collective alienation—like the apostle, we must speak the language of the day—is rooted in the heart of each man, but it also affects social structures. Seneca imagines that slavery appeared as a disturbance of nature. Irenaeus of Lyons (like all commentators on Paul) explains: 'When man was separated from God, he sank to such a degree of savagery that he regarded even members of his family as enemies.' The slavery of sin spares no-one. Seneca always suggests that certain men are more capable of reason, that they are more able than others to master their passions and attain true freedom. One of the first Christian philosophers, Clement of Alexandria, retorts, quoting Plato, that vice enslaves and that we are all slaves of sin. This levelling down shatters any hierarchy.

But to proclaim the Christian hope, redemption by him who took on the form of a slave (Phil. 2:7), Paul and a whole Christian literature continue to use the vocabulary of the slave-owning society. Let us cite another witness, Justin, a philosopher turned Christian, settled in Rome (second century): 'It was to restore both free men and slaves . . . that Christ came, granting equal dignity to all who keep his commandments.' In commenting on this emancipation (another significant Pauline formula) preaching discovers a whole Old Testament spirituality exalting the poor man, the servant, who, by his obedience, deserved the special protection of God. Luke's Gospel (1:38) offers a model: 'Behold the handmaid of the Lord,' says Mary at the annunciation. There are clear signs that such language made an impact on the Christian people; the faithful begin to adopt the title 'slave of the Lord'. So Euelpistos, who belongs to the emperor, declares to the prefect of Rome that he is a Christian, a freedman of Christ, once a slave of Caesar, now a slave of Christ. This reply is sufficient to indicate the critical force of Christian preaching. In this ancient society in which the sense of the sacred is being reborn after an eclipse, the brotherhood of man is of divine right. Whereas slavery, as a system, belongs to evil, the image of the slave (like that of the poor man) enters history to provide an example of humility in the service of God. The philosophers confide their reflections to a group of inmates, but the message of Paul and his successors reverberates through the whole Mediterranean basin, echoed by pastors and missionaries.

2. A SOCIAL TEACHING?

Do these revolutionary principles imply a social teaching, a policy of abolition? Before we accuse the propagators of the new religion of idealism, we must scrutinise the pagan philosophers and lawyers who denounce slavery but participate more or less directly in power. The numbers of the slave population, which had become enormous in Italy at the time of the great conquests, certainly decreased in the second century. The empire, by now more or less stabilised, had stopped ravaging new nations, and the flow of captives thrown on to the slave market had begun to dry up. The market had to rely on commercial importation, on the traffic in sold or abandoned children, and on the banned practices of the kidnapper. The raising of a human livestock probably did not compensate for the strength of a powerful trend of emancipation established in Roman society by the collective behaviour of masters. This evolution, which probably did not depend on philosophical propaganda (and which we shall not try to analyse) could have encouraged a policy of abolition. However, the influence of Stoicism, operating from the second century through the lawyers, never had sufficient weight to end the system. Its achievements include humanitarian legislation prohibiting abuses such as the sending of dependants to the brothel or the beasts, condemning the savagery of masters who mutilated or murdered their servants. The law, in some cases, made the procedures of emancipation more flexible; it did not free the slaves, all the slaves.

Paul did not preach abolition any more than Seneca; it is not even certain—if we keep to the obscure testimony of 1 Cor. 7:21—that he encouraged emancipation. Certainly the pastors and moralists of the second century did not make it obligatory for a convert master to free his slaves. Was this the indifference of spiritual men who neglected the present because they believed the end of the ages to be very near? Apparently not; it tended to be the sects, intoxicated by the hope of an imminent end, who preached the destruction of social structures. The propaganda for the emancipation of slaves only appears late, in hagiographic literature in the time of the Christian empire; at the time, Paul's silence became an alibi for social conservatism. In the early centuries, however, under an appearance of great caution, Christian preaching sketched out a whole system of rules with a bearing, indirect perhaps but nonetheless real, on the slave system. It condemned the circus games at which slave blood flowed. With Clement of Alexandria, it borrowed from the pagan moralists' diatribe to belabour the excesses of luxury, which crowded rich houses with slaves. In addition, however, it spoke the language of the Bible to celebrate the irreplaceable virtue of work, which made the services of an army of slaves redundant. More firmly, there was a ban on all trafficking which supplied the slave market, the abandonment of children, the sale of human beings like cattle. The churches did not exclude slave-owners from their communities, but, without exception, they excluded kidnappers (1 Tim. 1:10) and all dealers in human beings. Do the prescriptions of this social morality seem partial? They illustrate the specific image Christians had of slavery. All they knew well was the slavery of the towns, of their luxury and their pleasures. It was to take another two centuries before missionary activity really left the city and discovered the wretched population of the countryside. Such, in outline is the geography of the practical influence exercised by the critique and morality of the Christians.

The social composition of the first communities also contributed to the crystallising of habits, the fixing of attitudes. Let us immediately get rid of a legend which claims that at the beginning Christianity was a slave religion. Responsibility for this illusion lies with a pagan polemicist of the second century, Celsus; for him, this religion professed by illiterate preachers could attract only women and slaves. In fact—as F. Bömer's recent study shows—slaves generally practised the same cults as their masters; certainly they did not specially seek out a God whose humility mirrored their own dependence. The poverty of our sources hardly allows us to recover with any certainty the sociology of the early Christian groups, but all the evidence suggests that in the early days slaves were often converted at the same time as their masters. Onesimus, the servant who sought refuge with Paul, belonged to the Christian Philemon. In his letter to the Romans, Paul sends greetings to the 'house' of Narcissus, i.e., to the free men with their slaves. In Corinth, according to Acts, Crispus, the 'ruler of the synagogue', adopted the faith with all his house (Acts 18:8).

This last example suggests another remark, this time about masters. Historians have too often speculated on the influence of the Stoics while forgetting the influence which may have been exercised by the Jewish Christians. This point has all the more force since Judaism had prepared the way for the Christian challenge and offered, in minute detail, an original model of behaviour. In the third century the Christian Origen could still praise the Jewish law on servitude, which he thought more just than the pagan system. The Jewish law distinguished between the Jewish slave and the 'Canaanite'. The former had to be freed in principle after six years during which he was carefully protected. The master was required to share work and food fraternally with him and, if necessary, take in his family. Anyone who bought a Jew bought a master, said the rabbis. And the law prohibited the sale of a son of Israel to a gentile and recommended the redemption of Jewish captives. With the Canaanite the attitude changes: the doctors of the Law did not particularly advise emancipation, but they ruled that the slave should be converted, on the ground that it was difficult to share daily life with gentiles. Once purified by the proselyte's bath, the slave was better protected since he was virtually a member of the community of the covenant.

3. AN ALTERNATIVE SOCIETY

Christianity gives the model of the new covenant with no more Jews or Greeks a free interpretation. Paul outlines the ideal of a fraternal community, a sort of alternative society which brings together the servants of God on an equal footing. Within their own number the churches abolished all social distinctions, more completely than the pagan colleges, more successfully than the synagogues. All the baptised took part in the mysteries around the president of the synaxis. It is true that the master was consulted when a slave asked for baptism, but this practice can be explained by the generally evidenced wish to test every candidacy by means of a sort of sponsorship. The precaution is less easy to explain if the master is a pagan, and the practice of the churches differs here; some, in the West, defy the owner's opposition, while others, more anxious not to mix social conflicts with conversion, show a curious respect for the master's power. However, this is no more than a discord, because baptism wipes out all distinctions and the churches show no hesitation in recruiting their ministers from among slaves. The career of Pope Callistus is a spectacular example of this social advancement made possible by a church appointment. The servant of an imperial freedman, the future bishop was given the task of opening a more or less legal finance office. Deported to Sardinia because the business went wrong, he returned with the aura of a martyr. On becoming a deacon he organised the Church's burial ground, which accepted all burials without distinction. This former slave gave pastoral work a more egalitarian outlook. This is well illustrated by his agreement as a bishop to legitimise—from the point of view of Christian ethics—the stable union of a free woman with a Christian slave. Callistus was concerned to preserve the moral life of aristocrats who refused a pagan partner of their own rank and could not officially contract such an unequal alliance without losing their rank. To avoid a spiritual misalliance, he did not worry about the laws and gave equal consideration to the free woman and the slave. Never had Christian discipline so clearly attempted to establish, on the fringe of civil society, a community governed by its own laws.

Callistus' regulations could apply only—as we noted—within households which were already Christian, and these provided the means whereby the community built up outside the secular city could find some sort of place in the world. It was also within these domestic groups that Christian pastoral action was concerned to transform the relations of masters and slaves who were united in the brotherhood of a common faith. Paul returned to his Christian master Philemon the runaway slave Onesimus, to whom the law forbade him to give refuge, 'no longer as a slave but as a brother'. More specifically, the literature of the second and third centuries lists a casuistry of duties imposed on the master reminiscent of that of the rabbis in their commentary on the Jewish law of slavery. The master is responsible for protecting and educating his slaves and for supervising their morals. Even more than the rabbi, the Christian pastor invited the master to convert the pagan slave, in short, to establish the little sheltered groups in which the brotherhood of the Church could take shape. Slaves received instructions to be humble and obedient; in all the manuals of discipline (the Didache), in all the pastoral letters (the Epistle of Barnabas), in all the treatises (Tertullian's or Clement of Alexandria's), these are the necessary counterpart of the paternalism demanded of the master. It is barely possible to write the history of these little societies in more detail; we must not be too optimistic. At the beginning of the fourth century the Spanish council of Elvira imposed a lengthy penance on a mistress who had beaten her maid to death. In addition the clergy continued to exercise supervision, and we may suppose that in general the condition of a slave in a Christian household resembled to some extent the life of a slave in Jewish households which is described in more detail in the Talmudic literature.

4. THE MARTYR SLAVE

For the rest we need only mention the condition of a Christian in the service of a pagan master. Subjected in his work and in his person to the will and caprices of his or her master, he or she risked the workhouse or being sent to a brothel if he or she intended to remain faithful to their moral commitment. The virgin Potamienna, we are told, preferred to be plunged into boiling pitch rather than yield to her master's advances. Another danger arose when the master became worried by the missionary zeal of his slaves. Celsus is already reporting such cases, and Tertullian records the fury of a pagan husband who sent to the workhouse a slave who had converted his mistress to an unduly rigid conjugal morality. Generally, life in a pagan household was difficult for Christians forced to deny themselves the consolations which lessened the rigours of servile life, the pleasures of the spectacles and promiscuity. The Christian communities also felt themselves under a particular obligation to help them, like the synagogues in the case of Jewish captives. They stood by the poor, the widows, the orphans, those permanent prisoners the slaves, and often recommended their redemption. At the beginning of the second century, Clement of Rome refers to the devotion of believers who sell themselves to pay the ransom. In the middle of the century the author of an apocalypse, Hermas, advises the Romans: 'Instead of buying fields, buy men free. . . .' In this city the Church possessed a charitable fund supported by collections, and this may have been the origin of the practice of emancipation in the community, *in ecclesia*, which was legitimised in the fourth century by the law of the Christian empire. But the increasing number of slave conversions eventually made it impossible to make the purchase of their freedom the norm, and pastors like Ignatius of Antioch advised against it where it might encourage interested and insincere slave conversions. At all events the pastoral epistles (1 Tim. 6; 2 Pet. 2:18) are already mentioning the condition of these slaves, for which 1 Peter, like Hermas later, uses the image of the witness or the suffering just man. The churches recommended patience and obedience to these slaves as to others, but they called on them to resist when what was at stake was their commitment to the faith. History—the history of the authentic *acta*—has not preserved many names for this martyrology. One reason is that slaves most often escaped the State persecution which struck free men. A few names have survived oblivion, such as Blandina of Lyons, martyred in a pogrom at the end of the second century. With this testimony we must certainly stop our analysis of Christian influence, with its ambivalent character: there are the silences and the examples of caution. Nevertheless this minority bears within it the seeds of a challenge undoubtedly more radical than the critique of the philosophers. With it the slave, the freedman and slave of the Lord, at least enters the history of the Church, in much the same way as he was already present in the Bible and in the life of the synagogues.

Translated by Francis McDonagh

Short Bibliography

On ancient slavery Westermann, W. L. *The Slave Systems of Greek and Roman Antiquity* (Philadelphia 1955) and the monographs of Vogt, J. especially *Sklaverei und Humanität. Studien zur antiken Sklaverei und ihrer Erforschung* (*Historia* supplements) (Wiesbaden 1968).

The old book by Allard, P. *Les Esclaves chrétiens depuis les premiers temps de l'eglise* (Paris 1876), has been criticised by Harnack, Jonkers, Marc Bloch and Verlinden.

For the early centuries see now Gülzow, H. *Christentum und Sklaverei in den ersten drei Jahrhunderten* (Bonn 1969).

For law Imbert, J. 'Réflexions sur le Christianisme et l'esclavage en droit romain' *Rev. Int. des Droits de l'Antiquité* 2 (1949) 445-475.

On marriage Gaudemet, J. 'La Décision de Calliste en matière de mariage' in *Studi U. E. Paoli* (Florence 1955) pp. 332-344.

On the persecutions Scheele, J. *Zur Rolle der Unfreien in den römischen Christenverfolgungen* (Tübingen 1970).

Bernhard Blumenkranz

Relations between Jews and Christians in the Eleventh Century

ALTHOUGH we always recommend that a study of relations between Jews and Christians should, in part at least, be comparative in method, the position this article is to occupy makes it difficult to follow that practice here. There can be no valid comparison between the attitudes we shall now be discussing and the Christian attitude to slaves in the fourth century or to the 'savages' discovered in the New World in the sixteenth century. The difference between them is one of kind, not of degree. To show the extent of the difference, we need only point out that whereas Christians have never been tempted to become slaves or savages, they have frequently been strongly attracted to Jews and Judaism. A common attitude of reverence for the Bible is the immediate explanation for this magnetic power of Judaism. But having the Old Testament in common—with differing attitudes towards it—has always underlain relations between Jews and Christians, even when the attraction gave way to bitter conflict.

An important element in the Christian attitude to Jews has been the low social esteem in which the latter were held, and Jules Isaac, in his impassioned study of Jewish-Christian relations, quite rightly placed great weight on it. Indeed, he showed a true historian's intuition when he called the last volume of his study *L'Enseignement du mépris*.[1] In the *Petit Robert* dictionary,[2] the first definition of the noun *mépris* (scorn, contempt) uses the word *indigne* (unworthy (i.e., of attention)); conversely, *indigne* is defined with recourse to *mépris*. So the term *mépris* in Isaac's title implies a social evaluation we would not wish to dispute.

However, we cannot accept Isaac's main argument that the Christian attitude to Jews remained almost unchanged from the second century until the first half of the twentieth. Rather, as this article will show, our own position comes closer to that of Lea Dasberg in her *Untersuchungen über die Entwertung des Judenstatus im 11. Jahrhundert*.[3] The use of the word *Entwertung* (devaluation, degrading) suggests clearly tha she sees the history of Jewish-Christian relations as being to some extent a process of change and development, and we readily agree with her that, running right through the eleventh century, the foreshadowings of a change can be seen.

But the change itself occurred in its entirety as a result of the first crusade; similarly, it was the crusade which made it evident that the change had taken place. For our present purpose we may disregard the immense importance of the crusades both in general history and, more particularly, in the history of Western Christianity. But in the history of Western Jews, the first crusade—or indeed, the first year of that crusade—quite undeniably marks a major turning-point. Jewish tradition recognises this fact by singling out the year 1096 for special attention. In Hebrew, where, as the reader will recall, letters act also as figures, TaTNU has come to symbolise the change. We may therefore legitimately centre our study on this one particular year, though we shall of course seek points of comparison both earlier and later.

In 1096 itself, and more markedly from that year on, there is a fundamental change in the Christian attitude to Jews, but there is a fundamental change also in the Jewish attitude to Christians. For this reason, and since our subject is the reciprocal relations between the two groups, we have chosen the most economical approach open to us and based our study on the Hebrew chronicle which gives most details about the first crusade. It was written, or to be more accurate, written up by Salomon bar Simeon.[4]

Before we examine in detail the events of 1096, however, we shall turn back to the earlier eleventh century and the foreshadowings of change mentioned three paragraphs ago.

1. THE FIRST GREAT PERSECUTION OF 1007-1011

At the very beginning of the century, between 1007 and 1011, there occurred the first geographically widespread persecution of the Jews. It has been suggested, and rightly so, that this widespread persecution could be seen as a distant forerunner of the crusades.[5] In fact it foreshadows them in two ways. First, the bitterness which the destruction of the church of the Holy Sepulchre provoked among Christians in the West reveals the concern they felt for the historic Christian monuments in Palestine. Second, the persecution shows the Christians attempting to find, close to home, a scapegoat on whom that crime could be blamed until such time as they could fulfil their albeit unconscious expectations and go to Palestine to ensure the safety both of the monuments and of the pilgrims who wished to visit them. Raoul Glaber is our main Christian source here.[6] According to him, the church of the Holy Sepulchre was destroyed on the orders of 'the prince of Babylon' (the Caliph El-Hakim), but at the instigation of the Jews! The Jews of Orleans, he reports, who were 'more violent, envious and rash than the rest of the Jewish people', wrote to the Caliph to tell him that unless he destroyed this venerable building, the Christians would come and take over his kingdom. When the Jews' crime became known, 'it was decided unanimously by the Christians that the Jews should be expelled from the countries and towns where they lived. Thus, universally hated, they were driven from the towns; others were put to the sword, drowned in the rivers or otherwise tortured to death; some also took their own lives in various ways. The bishops then decided also that Christians should be forbidden to have any relations or dealings with them. Nevertheless, if some of the Jews agreed to be baptised, and to put aside all Jewish habits and customs, then they and they alone should be admitted to baptism.'

We are fortunate in that there is another narrative of these same events, from a Jewish source.[7] According to this text, the persecution of the Jews was confined to France; it was decided on by the king, Robert the Pious, and his councillors, and obliged the Jews to choose between conversion and death. The only justification put forward was that their 'customs and Law are different from those of all other peoples'. As we see, there is here no mention of the accusation reported by Raoul Glaber that the Jews were in collusion with the Muslims. Was the Jewish writer perhaps better informed than Glaber, as the use of modern historical methods would suggest? A recent study has certainly shown that the accusation of Jewish collusion with the Caliph is nonsensical, since he was as savagely opposed to the Jews as to the Christians.[8]

2. THE PERSECUTION AT THE BEGINNING OF THE FIRST CRUSADE, 1066

We move now to the end of the eleventh century and the persecution of the Jews in 1096. Once again we shall turn first to a Christian writer, Guibert de Nogent, to discover the reasons alleged for the persecution. He recounts as follows what happened in Rouen on January 26 1096: 'Those who had put on the cross and so committed themselves to taking part in the crusade began to complain among themselves: "We are prepared to travel a long way in order to fight the enemies of God in the East, yet here under our very eyes we have Jews, whose people are the greatest possible enemy of God. Why not start at the beginning, rather than the end?'' So saying, they first took up arms, then drove (the Jews) ... into a church, and put them to the sword regardless of age or sex, though in such a way that those who agreed to submit to the law of Christ escaped death.' It is noteworthy that in Salomon bar Simeon's Hebrew chronicle we find almost the same words: 'When (the crusaders') road took them through towns where there were Jews, one would say to the other: "Look, we are going a long distance to reach the church of the Holy Sepulchre and take revenge on the Ismaelites, and yet here, living in our very midst, are the Jews whose fathers killed him (Jesus) and crucified him. Let us punish them first and wipe them from the face of the earth, so that the very name of Israel falls into oblivion. Or else let them, like us, confess Jesus as the Lord".' (Hl; G82).[10]

As we have seen, at the beginning of the eleventh century the Jews were accused—rightly or wrongly—of a crime that was both recent and specific. At the time of the first crusade, by contrast, they were accused either of the long-past crime of 'deicide', or, what is worse, not of a crime at all but of a state: that of being Jewish. In both cases, it was open to them to escape death by accepting baptism. The persecution early in the century was attributed either to a unanimous agreement of the whole Christian body, backed up by a decision of all the bishops, or to an order by the king in his council. At the time of the crusade, the persecution is reported to have sprung from a spontaneous decision by the people, made this time without reference to any authority. But neither did the authorities make any real stand against it.

The persecution early in the century was not followed through. A prominent Rouen Jew, Jacob bar Yekutiel, stating that the pope alone had the power to order such a measure, protested against it, and announced his intention of going to see the pope and seeking his opinion. The Duke of Normandy, Richard II the Good, gave him permission to make the journey. He was heard in audience by John XVIII, to whom he complained that in France, a kingdom subject to papal authority, many Jews had been killed and others forced to become Christians, all without papal authorisation. The pope more than met Jacob bar Yekutiel's hopes, since he not only despatched a message to France, but also sent a bishop as legate to end the persecution.[11]

For the time of the 1096 crusade, we know of only one appeal to high authority. Following a rumour that Godefroy de Bouillon had taken a vow to attack the Jews before leaving for the crusade, the head of the Jewish community in Mainz appealed to the Emperor Henry IV for protection. Henry immediately ordered all princes, bishops, counts and dukes, to protect the Jews (H3; G87-8). Could it be because of this appeal to the Emperor, who at the time was still a faithful supporter of the antipope Clement III, that Urban II uttered not a single word in condemnation of the threatened persecution? Indeed, did the pope stop short at silence? Salomon bar Simeon gives a most hostile account of the speech appealing for the crusade that Urban II made at Clermont: 'Then there appeared the Prince of Darkness, the pope of Rome the Evil, who called upon all the peoples who believe in Jesus . . .' (H4;G89). The harsh criticisms Salomon makes at some points gain credence from his fulsome expressions of gratitude when he has any cause to be grateful. Thus, for example, when he writes of Johann, Bishop of Speyer, his gratitude is total, even though the bishop had been unable to prevent the killing of eleven members of the Jewish community during the first assault by the crusaders, on May 18 (H2;G84). After that, however, the bishop had managed to ensure that the Jews were fully protected; so much so, indeed, that his protection was extended to some survivors from the terrible slaughter in Mainz, whom he welcomed with the promise that he would 'watch over them as a father watches over his child'. And in gratitude Salomon ends the short passage he devotes to the bishop by exclaiming: 'May his memory be blest and exalted for ever!' (H31;G142-3).

In contrast, however, if a bishop or archbishop failed to keep an initial promise of assistance, then the higher his rank, the harsher the criticism. The Archbishop of Mainz, for example, had let the Jews in the town deposit all their money in his treasury, and had agreed to harbour them in his palace. But all that, says the chronicle bitterly, was done only in order to 'gain power over us, and then to trap us like fish caught in an evil net' (H3;G86. see Eccles. 9:12). The complaint was justifiable, for when Emicho of Leimingen, the Jews' fiercest enemy, arrived with his hordes, the archbishop announced his intention of going on a pastoral visitation in the country. The Jewish leaders had to insist very powerfully—and make more gifts of money—before he agreed to remain in Mainz. He then made another promise, in which he was joined by the count: 'We shall either die with you, or ensure that you live' (H5;G93). But, in the end, he proved to be unwilling to risk his own life, since he fled as soon as he was personally threatened by the crusaders (H6;G95).

The Archbishop of Cologne, Hermann III, evacuated the Jews of Cologne to seven places of asylum, but the town of Kerpen was the only one of the seven in which they were not massacred by the crusaders. Yet even there they had cause to complain of the wickedness of the Governor, who had sent his servants to Cologne to remove the gravestones from the Jewish cemetery (H25;G131). The Jews could not but see this action as implying that the Jewish community of Cologne had permanently ceased to exist, and that all its possessions were to be disposed of to the first bidder, as if they had now no legal owner nor heir.

To be savagely slaughtered by the crusaders—to have their throats slit like sacrificial lambs, to be strangled or drowned, to be burned or stoned to death or buried alive—was seen by the Jews as being so to speak in the order of things, despite the refinements of torture used in inflicting the different forms of death (H23;G127). When corpses were profaned—stripped naked, dragged over the ground, or left without burial—reaction was stronger. But the defilement they felt most deeply, perhaps because until 1096 it had not occurred since the seventh century, was the desecration of synagogues and especially of the scrolls of the Torah.

If the synagogues had been safe from attack since the seventh century, it was less by virtue of the provisions of Roman law than because Gregory the Great had reaffirmed those provisions.[12] To understand St Gregory's motives, we must turn to a theological tradition deriving from St Augustine, and bear in mind the essential relation between the synagogue and the reading of Scripture. According to Augustine, the Jewish people must necessarily survive until the coming of the Last Days in order to bear witness to the truth of Christianity by means of the biblical texts which had been given into its safekeeping.[13] This theory had been so thoroughly assimilated into the common body of Christian thought that it came eventually to be referred to without mention of Augustine. The same process occurred with the *herbraica veritas*, the Hebrew text of the Bible; St Jerome through his translation was the first to give it full recognition in the West, after which reference to it became common practice, at least among scholars. In the early middle ages, then, as this excursus reminds us, Christians held the Hebrew Bible in the deepest respect.

But not so the crusaders in 1096. In Trier, on April 10, not content with stealing the gold and silver adornments, they tore up the scrolls of the Torah, threw them on the ground, trampled them underfoot (H25-6;G132). In Worms, on May 18, they dragged them through the mud and burned them (H2;G84). The height of sacrilege was reached in Cologne, with the desecration taking place on June 1, the Jewish day of Pentecost, the very feast which celebrates the giving of the Law to Israel (H18;G117).

3. THE REACTION OF THE JEWS

For all the acts of violence and outrages against them, the Jews never wavered in their trust in God. Their attitude in 1096 alone would justify their being called 'obstinate', since they invoked the indescribable persecution which took place that year to claim that they were more than ever the people beloved of God: 'This generation has been chosen by Him to become His inheritance, for they had the strength and the power to remain faithful to His Temple, to fulfil His word and to sanctify His great name in His world' (H2;G83).

It must also be said, however, that the Jewish attitude to the persecution was not invariably one of proud but passive suffering; there are many examples of armed riposte which could be quoted (see H6,10,15-16, 28-9; G95-5,103,112-13, 137-8). But they were too far outnumbered to defend themselves by arms, so turned instead to the twin weapons of any minority group which is both proud and weak: vituperation, and appeals for divine vengeance.

The vituperation was aimed at the most visible symbols of Christianity: the cross, the church, baptism, Jesus and the Virgin Mary, the crusade and the crusaders. An attempt has been made to justify this verbal abuse on the grounds that medieval Jews found the use of Christian terms repugnant, but the author's concern was more apologetic than scientific.[14] In fact, earlier Jewish texts either show no such scruple, or overcome the difficulty by using perfectly acceptable periphrases. As for the second weapon, the calls for divine vengeance, they become more frequent the worse the bloodshed has been, in both the number and the quality of its victims. To close his account of the persecution in Mainz, in which more than eleven hundred Jews were killed, Salomon bar Simeon fills nearly two pages of his text with such appeals (H16-17;G114-15). Appropriate quotations from Scripture predominate: 'Then He will judge the nations for the numbers they have slain' (Ps. 110:6);[15] 'Praise His people, O you nations; for He avenges the blood of His servants' (Deut. 32:43); 'O Lord, thou God of vengeance, thou God of vengeance, shine forth!' (Ps. 94:1); 'Exact sevenfold retribution of our neighbours for their outrage' (Ps. 94:2); 'Pour out Thy anger on the nations that do not know Thee, and on the kingdoms that do not call on Thy name!' (Ps. 79:6); 'Pour out Thy indignation upon them, and let Thy burning anger overtake them' (Ps. 69:24). It is vengeance in the present, not in some distant future, that is called for. At times, we hear the words of those who are about to die: 'May the God of mercy avenge His servants in the lifetime of those who survive us; before their very eyes He avenge the blood that has been and will yet be spilt' (H22;G125).

If a persecutor of the Jews is struck by misfortune the chronicler is jubilant: 'Thus the zeal of the God of justice shows that He exacted retribution for their evil deeds. May He now soon, in our time, avenge the blood of His servants . . .' (H25;G131). He stays within the bounds of the Germanic empire to recount the sufferings of the Jews, but ranges far and wide to follow the downfall of those who inflicted their suffering: 'They were overthrown, and when we learnt of it we rejoiced, for the Lord has wrought vengeance on our enemies and wiped them from the face of the earth' (H29-30;G138-40).

The material we have been examining so far will have made amply clear why the Jews adopted an attitude of non-involvement with the crusade.

But their failure to join it was not only an accidental circumstance of the persecution; it was also one of its causes. An anecdote told by Salomon bar Simeon but found also in two Christian accounts illustrates this point. Among the crusaders in Mainz, runs the story, was a woman who had with her a goose that followed her everywhere. 'Look,' she said to the passers-by, 'my goose understood me when I spoke of going to the tomb of Jesus, so it decided to come with me too.' Hearing this, the crusaders began to attack the Jews (H4;G90-91). Though the story is elliptical, its purpose is quite clear: everyone, mindless animals as well as men, was going on the crusade; the Jews alone were taking no part in it.

It should be explained that the crusade represents the first occasion on which the Jews did not participate in a foreign war waged by western nations. In 1063, for example, the soldiers going to reconquer Spain from the Moors had begun attacking Jews, but the Spanish bishops, with those of what is now South and South-East France, forbade the attacks, and were congratulated on their stand by the pope, Alexander II.[16] There was a profound difference, wrote the pope in an order, between the Saracens and the Jews. It was permissible to make war on the former, since they hunted down Christians and drove them from the towns, but not on the Jews, who were always willing to serve.

In 1096, no such papal condemnation was forthcoming. And thousands of Jews lost their lives because, as was really only natural, they would have no part in the crusade. But their non-participation had a yet graver outcome, since from it stemmed the ever more marked social isolation which, for the Jews, prolonged the middle ages until the French Revolution. Then, scarcely two centuries ago, it was the Abbé Grégoire, a Christian, and indeed a cleric—but a lone voice amid clerics and Christians alike—who took the first major step towards bringing the Jewish people out of its medieval isolation. The churches waited rather longer.

Translated by Ruth Murphy

Notes

1. Paris 1962 (E.T.: *The Teaching of Contempt—Christian Roots of Anti-semitism* [New York 1964]).

2. Paul Robert *Dictionnaire alphabétique et analogique de la langue française* 2nd ed. (Paris 1978).

3. The Hague 1965.

4. A. Neubauer and M. Stern *Hebräische Berichte über die Judenverfolgungen während der Kreuzzüge*, ins Deutsche übersetzt von S. Baer (Quellen z. Gesch. der Juden in Deutschl 2) (Berlin 1892) pp. 1-31 and 81-143.

5. C. Erdmann *Die Entstehung des Kreuzzugsgedankens* (Stuttgart 1935).

6. See B. Blumenkranz *Les Auteurs chrétiens latins du moyen âge sur les juifs et le judaïsme* (Paris and The Hague 1963) pp. 256-259 and the editions listed there.

7. A. M. Habermann, ed. *Sefer gezerot Ashkenaz we-Zarfat* (Jerusalem 1945/6) pp. 19-21.

8. See M. Canard 'Hakim' in *Encyclopédie de l'Islam*² 3' (Leyden and Paris 1971) pp. 79-84.

9. G. Bourin, ed. *De Vita Sua* II 5 (Paris 1907) pp. 118-120.

10. See note 4. In the references, the first figure refers to the Hebrew text, the second to the German translation.

11. See B. Blumenkranz *Juifs et chrétiens dans le monde occidental* (The Hague and Paris 1960) p. 136 and note 252.

12. See B. Blumenkranz 'Synagogues en France du haut moyen âge' *Archives Juives* 14 (1978) 40.

13. See B. Blumenkranz 'Augustin et les juifs, Augustin et le judaïsme' *Recherches Augustiniennes* 1 (1958) 231-232.

14. Thus H. Bresslau in the introduction to *Hebräische Berichte* (see note 4 above) p. xxvii.

15. This translation and that given for Ps. 94:2 are based on the French versions in the original text of the article, which differ from modern English translations, both Jewish and Christian. The remaining quotations from the Bible are given according to the Revised Standard Version.

I am grateful to Dr E. Isaacson for his help with this and other points (Translator's note).

16. See B. Blumenkranz *Auteurs* (see note 6 above) pp. 263-264.

Enrique Dussel

Modern Christianity in Face of the 'Other'

(From the 'Rude' Indian to the 'Noble Savage')

MAN possesses 'dignity' intrinsically, through being a human person; there is nothing in all creation more dignified than the human person. However, throughout history all systems of oppression have deprived of 'dignity' all those who are either the oppressed 'within' the system, or enemies, barbarians, *goim*, the 'senseless', those 'outside' the system: those who *are not*. Everywhere outside the system reigns 'civilisation's' night, the shapeless mass which, for the system, represents impending danger, the demoniacal. This pattern has always been present in history, but now we must analyse it briefly as it is to be seen in the process of European expansion from the fifteenth century onwards, since America was discovered in 1492 and the Pilgrim Fathers reached the shores of North America in 1620. The subject is a highly topical one.

1. THE FACTS OF THE CASE

In 1577, before Italy, Germany, France or England had seen beyond the merely European horizon, José de Acosta published in Lima (Peru), in the introduction to his work *De procuranda indorum salute* (or *Predicación del Evangelio en las Indias*), a typology of three categories of 'barbarians': 'Although these peoples are of many different provinces, nations and qualities, yet it seems to me, after long and careful consideration, that they can be reduced to three very diverse classes or categories, which embrace all barbarian nations.'[1]

In a general sense, 'barbarians' means[2] 'those who reject true reason and the way of life commonly accepted among men, and who thus display barbarian *roughness* (rudeza), barbarian savagery'.[3] Of course, for every European down to the present day, 'true reason' and 'the commonly accepted way of life' are *his own*, by which others are judged and condemned as less than human, as we shall see shortly. José de Acosta suggests that the Chinese, the Japanese and the peoples of other parts of the East Indies, though they are barbarians, should be treated 'in much the same way as the apostles treated the Greeks and Romans in preaching to them'.[4] So far as these 'stable republics, with public laws and fortified towns' are concerned, says Acosta, 'if one tried to bring them into submission to Christ by force and with arms, one would only succeed in rendering them exceedingly hostile to the name of Christian'.[5]

A second type of barbarian consists of such as the Aztecs or Incas, who though they are well known for their political and religious institutions, 'have not attained to the use of writing or to the knowledge of philosophy'.[6] These are, as it were, in the middle of the road.

Finally we come to 'the third category of barbarians'; 'This is composed of savages resembling wild beasts. . . . And in the New World there are countless herds of them. . . . They differ very little from animals. . . . It is necessary to teach these people who are hardly men, or who are half men, how to become men, and to instruct them like children. . . . They must be held down by force . . . and, in a way, even against their will, they must be compelled (Acosta quotes Luke 14:23) to enter the kingdom of heaven.'[7]

All this in spite of the fact that José de Acosta was a defender of the Indians and a famous theologian who did not accept the thesis of Ginés de Sepúlveda. Even so he was unable to avoid contamination by the ideology of his time, unable to free himself from a humanistic Eurocentrism. The temporal Messianism of Spain and Portugal led on to those of Holland in the seventeenth century, of France and England from the eighteenth century onwards, of Germany in the nineteenth century and of north America in recent decades.

Feudal Europe made its first attempt at expansion by conquest with the crusades, but the Arab world resisted this first act of European aggression perpetrated in the name of Christianity. The second expansion, also in the name of Christianity, began in the fifteenth century, not in the Eastern Mediterranean but across the Atlantic and Indian Oceans. Pierre Chaunu even says that 'the sixteenth century brought about, from our point of view, the greatest mutation in the human species'.[8] From that moment on, the citizen—who for Aristotle was 'political man'—is the one who inhabits the European city; the *civis*, or civilised person, displayed *civilitas*, or 'conduct becoming to the citizen'—*civilisation*. 'Man' is, for the European, the European citizen, just as he was for the aristocrat Aristotle under a system which practised slavery. Gonzalo Fernández de

Oviedo (1478-1557), writing more as a European than as a Spaniard, said in his *Historia General y natural de las Indias*: 'These people of the Indies, though they are rational and descended from the same stock that came out of Noah's sacred ark, have become *irrational and bestial* by reason of their idolatries, sacrifices and infernal ceremonies.'[9]

And along the same lines Ginés de Sepúlveda explains: 'The fact of having cities and some sort of rational manner of life and some kind of commerce is something brought about by natural necessity, and it only serves to prove that they are not bears or monkeys, and that they are not totally lacking in reason.'[10]

For Europeans, for Spaniards, 'the other', the native, was a *rudo*. The word is derived from the Latin *rudis* (in the rough, not having been worked on), from the verb *rudo* (to bray, to roar). It is the opposite to 'erudite' and erudition (which indicate the one who has no roughness, brutishness, lack of cultivation). Even the best Europeans thought of the Indian as a 'rudo', a 'child', a piece of educable, evangelisable 'material'. 'Christendom' was beginning its glorious expansion, and papal bulls gave theological justification to the plundering of the peoples of the Third World.

2. THEOLOGICAL PREMISSES

Every theology becomes a 'theology of domination' when it expresses theoretically, with the support of theological arguments, the interests of the dominant class of a nation which practises oppression. Such a 'theology of domination' can argue its case logically with great coherence. In the first place, the system, the totality (the 'flesh', *basar* in Hebrew) is made into a fetish, becomes totalitarian, comes to see itself as an absolute, as the ultimate, before which the Utopia of a later and better system is judged to be demoniacal, illegitimate, atheistic. The Israelites themselves, whether as a result of ideological contamination from neighbouring nations and empires, or as a development occurring during the period of the monarchy, use the category of *goim*[11] to indicate those peoples who are barbarian, foreign, inferior. 'Hellenicity', *romanitas*, Christendom, European *civilisation* are concepts which involve the same fetishistic absolutising of the totality, of the system. These concepts are the top layer of the theology of domination. In essence this process of making into a fetish the dominant class of the nation which practices oppression is based on the denial of 'exteriority'[12] on the relegation of the *other* as such to a position where he is seen only as relative to the system. And it is in this that sin ultimately consists. To deprive the Other of the 'dignity' which is essentially and naturally his (*dignus* is the one who by being a person, whether 'Other' or not, is deserving of the highest respect:

he is *someone* distinct), means, primarily, to plunder him of his alterity (otherhood), of his liberty, of his humanity. Once the Other has been deprived of his divine exteriority (by means of the artifice of judging him to be a barbarian, non-man, a mere beast, the Enemy[13] *par exellence*) he can be manipulated, controlled, dominated, tortured, assassinated—and all this in the name of 'Being' (as old Schelling would say), or of 'civilisation', or of 'Christendom', of the totality elevated into a fetish. It is obvious that this negative judgment on the Other will lead immediately, because of the political and practical power of those who make it, to a limitation of his *material* possibilities in life. It is at the economic level— which still forms part of what is offered to God in worship, as in the Catholic *Offertorium*, which says: 'Through your goodness, we have this bread to offer, which earth has given and human hands have made'—that the deprivation of the Other is consummated. It is at this point that it becomes a *reality*. The Indian will not only be regarded as a 'beast', but he will be free manpower for a colonial tributary system which will be one of the main contributory factors to the original accumulation of European capital, beginning in the sixteenth century.

This is why, in times of prophetic activity or messianic expectation, this burden of negativity resting upon the *goim*, the pagans, the 'nations', is immediately lifted: 'I have put my spirit upon him, he will bring forth justice to the nations (*goim*)' (Isa. 42:1); 'When the Son of man comes in his glory . . . then he will sit on his glorious throne. Before him will be gathered all the nations (*ēthnē*)' (Matt. 25:31-32).[14]

A theology of domination fixes the 'frontiers' ('that my salvation may reach to the *end* (frontiers) of the earth', Isa. 49:6),[15] and declares the Other 'beyond' salvation, beyond being, beyond dignity. Liberation, on the other hand, goes beyond the horizon of the system and includes the Other as an equal, a brother, a member of the eschatological community.

3. THE DISPUTE OVER THE STATUS OF THE NATURE OF THE INDIAN

Theologically the dispute of 1550 in Valladolid between Juan Ginés de Sepúlveda and Bartolomé de las Casas is the most important that has ever taken place in Europe on the subject of the nature of man and cultures of the Third World, in terms of what a man is ontologically and what he is in the light of faith. Thereafter the question would not be re-opened until the theology of liberation appeared, well on into the twentieth century. We have to understand that theologically the Indians were helped, para- doxically, by a certain interplay of *classes* (although in practice they were to be oppressed politically and economically to the point of complete alienation). In effect the 'encomendero class' (those who received the tribute contributed by the Indians in the form of work) was organising itself into a powerful oligarchy in Spanish America (as was the slave-owning class in Brazil). The king could not lend his support to this 'encomendero class', because they had a tendency towards separatism—as the conquistadors had shown in Peru. Thus, paradoxically, the king would not permit the publication of the works of Ginés de Sepúlveda (which offered justification for the oppression of the Indian by the 'encomenderos' in America), and on the other hand would permit the publication of he works of Bartolomé de las Casas, which denied that the conquest had any proper foundation and established the Indian's right to freedom. The king needed to weaken the growing American oligarchy in order to buttress his own power. At this juncture, Bartolomé came out in criticism of the 'encomenderos' and sought the support of the king for the liberation of the Indians. 'For the first—and probably the last—time', says a north American author, 'a colonialist nation set up a genuine investigation into the justice of the methods employed to extend its domination'.[16] In fact, the Council of the Fourteen, the 'Council of the Indies', listened to the judgment of theologians before giving its opinions on the justice of the conquest.

Ginés de Sepúlveda based his theological arguments on many authors, among them Aristotle, John Major, Fernández de Oviedo, the Bull of Alexander VI, etc. Bartolomé argued passionately against the same authors.

Aristotle had affirmed that 'he who is a man not in virtue of his own nature but in virtue of that of another is by nature a slave. . . . Those who find obedience to authority advantageous to them are slaves by nature (*physei douloi*). . . . The usefulness of slaves differ little from that of animals'.[17] Ginés applied this doctrine to his theology of domination: 'There are other grounds for a just war against the Indians . . . and one of them is to subdue by arms, if no other way is possible, those who by reason of their natural condition ought to obey others but reject their rule.'[18]

The Scottish theologian John Major, for his part, had published in 1510 some *Commentaries on the Second Book of Sentences*, in which he referred to the territories recently discovered. Having said: 'If a certain people has embraced the faith of Christ, and has done so whole-heartedly, it is to be hoped that its rulers will be deposed from power if they persist in their paganism,'[19] he went on to write: 'There is something more to say. These peoples live as though they were beasts on both sides of the equator, and between the poles men live like wild beasts. And today all this has been discovered by experience.'[20]

To which Bartolomé de las Casas replies: 'Away, then, with John Major, seeing that he knows nothing at all of the law or of the facts! We have the ridiculous situation that this Scottish theologian comes and tells us that a king, even before he understands the Spanish language and even before he understands the reason why the Spaniards are building fortifications, should be deprived of his kingdom.'[21]

To Fernández de Oviedo, who argued that the Indians had fallen into
'bestial customs' and so found themselves incapable of receiving faith,
Bartolomé replied: 'Since Oviedo was a member of these perverse expeditions, what will he not say about the Indians? . . . Because of these brutal
crimes God has blinded his eyes,[22] along with those of the other plunderers, . . . so that he should not be able by the Grace of God to know that
these naked peoples were simple, good and pious.'[23]

So far as the Bulls of Alexander VI are concerned, Bartolomé analyses
the question and shows that the pope never justified war or violence as a
means of propagating the faith in the Indies. Queen Isabel herself
defended the Indians, and ordered that they should not 'be made to suffer
any kind of harm to their persons or their belongings'.[24]

It was in this way that in August and September 1550 Ginés and
Bartolomé were in confrontation with each other over the ability of the
Indians to receive the faith.

4. POSITION OF BARTOLOMÉ DE LAS CASAS

First as a conquistador, then as a young cleric, Bartolomé had a
particular respect for the Indian, whom he regarded as 'other': 'God
created each one of these widely scattered and innumerable people to be
of the utmost simplicity, without wickedness or duplicity, most obedient
and most loyal to their natural rulers and to the Christians whom they
serve. They are the most humble, most patient, most peaceful and docile,
and the most free from quarrels and bickering, to be found anywhere in
the world. Similarly they are extremely delicate peoples, slender and frail
in build, little able to support heavy labours and readily dying from almost
any illness.'[25]

It must be borne in mind that when Bartolomé exalts the Indian in this
manner he is in no way giving expression to the later myth of the *bon
sauvage*, the noble savage, much of which might well have had its inspiration in the *Brevīsima relación* itself. Bartolomé respected the Indian in
his *exteriority*. His language is at times stereotyped, as when he writes of
the Indians as 'so mild, so humble, so peaceful', but such an expression
shows precisely his ability to cross the frontier of the system and make
himself open to the *exteriority of the other as other*.

The arrival of the Spaniards in America was the first experience of the
'face-to-face' encounter: 'The Admiral (Columbus) and the others . . .
who now made the acquaintance of' the Indians[26] were confronting them
for the first time.

But immediately the Europeans attacked the Indians: 'As soon as they made their acquaintance, they hurled themselves upon them (the Indians), like the most cruel wolves,[27] tigers and lions, which had not eaten for many days. And for forty years from then until now (1552), they have done nothing but tear them to pieces, kill them, distress, afflict, torment and destroy them by strange, new, diverse forms of cruelty, the like of which have never been seen, read of or heard of.'[28]

Our prophetic *theologian of liberation* goes on building up his case against the alienation of the 'other'. He continues his discourse with a frontal attack on the *totality* of the European system of oppressive expansion: 'Convinced by the truth itself, he (the cleric Bartolomé de las Casas, in his autobiographical narrative) came to the conclusion that *everything* which was being done to the Indians in the Indies was unjust and tyrannical.'[29]

To Bartolomé, the greatest theologian of the sixteenth century, the whole system was unjust, starting with its basic intention: 'A hundred thousand victims have died and disappeared because of the labours which they (the Spaniards) out of their *lust for gold* imposed upon them.'[30] 'Out of their desire to have gold and wealth.'[31]

The God gold, the new fetish or idol of developing capitalism, was criticised by Bartolomé even when it was still in its cradle, when it had just been born. His critique of the modern European world—pre-capitalist, mercantile, capitalist, imperialist—had already begun. Along with Portugal and Spain he was criticising in anticipation Holland, England, France, and in our own time the 'Trilateral Empire' of the United States, Germany and Japan. The unjust notion of national prosperity was beginning its idolatrous reign: 'During the seventy years that have passed since they began to scandalise, rob, kill and extirpate those nations, *nobody to this day has pointed out* that so many things which are a scandal and shame to our holy faith, such robberies, injustices, ravages, killings, taking of captives, usurpation of the rights of nations and of others' right to rule, and, finally, such universal devastation and depopulation, *have been sinful and the greatest possible injustice*.'[32]

This explicit theologian of liberation was, in addition, an ideological theologian. Very intelligently he drew attention to the relation between theory and practice ('nobody to this day has pointed out', nobody has seen, discovered), and, above all, to the sin which was being committed with European expansion and oppression of other peoples. This is a theology of liberation which lays bare the ethico-theological perversity of colonialism and of the tributary economic system of the *encomienda*. To the present day European theology has ignored all this theology. It is time to revise history and remake it.

Bartolomé understood and expressed the dialectic of master and slave—two centuries before Rousseau and three before Hegel or

Marx—on a global scale. This is to be seen when he tells us that after the invaders had murdered all those who 'could long for, or sigh for, or think of liberty', a colonial order was set up 'which *oppressed them* with the most severe, horrible and harsh *servitude*'. In his *Testamento*, shortly before his death Bartolomé writes:

> God thought it right to choose me for his service though I did not deserve it, to campaign for all those peoples of the region we call the Indies . . . to *liberate them* (in the fine Spanish of the sixteenth century) from the violent death which they are still suffering.[33]

5. THE QUESTION OF THE 'NOBLE SAVAGE' IN TRIUMPHANT CAPITALISM

It was important to decide whether or not the Indian was capable of receiving the faith in order to justify or otherwise Spanish rule, and that of the 'encomendero' (the Creole who exploited the Indian as manpower), over the peoples of America. The discussion was set within the framework of capitalism in its early form, pre-industrial and mercantile. On the other hand, the question of the noble savage, at the end of the seventeenth and during the eighteenth centuries, was concerned with the right of Europeans (mainly the English and the French) to dominate the new colonies, but now within the framework of a capitalist system which was soon to be industrial (and, from the end of the nineteenth century, imperial). From a recent study we can see that 'Eurocentrism' and contempt for other peoples go hand-in-hand:

> Although Europe is the smallest of the three parts of *our* continent, it has nevertheless certain advantages which make it preferable to the *others*. Its air is extremely temperate and its provinces very fertile. . . . It excels by reason of its good properties and its peoples, who are normally mild, honest, civilised and much given to science and the arts. . . . The peoples of Europe, by reason of their education and their valour, have brought into submission *other* parts of the world. Their spirit is apparent in their works, their wisdom in their systems of government, their power in their arms, their standards of conduct in their commerce, and their magnificence in their cities. Thus in every respect Europe surpasses the *other* parts of the world. . . . In *our* view it is only right that the name of Europe should frequently be confused with that of Christianity.[34]

What is 'ours' means what is European, civilised, Christian; it means honest, strong people, gifted in science and the arts. The 'others' are pagans, foreigners, barbarians, without proper government and without faith. Bernard Duchene, going through the various articles in the *Dic-*

tionary to which we have referred one by one, discovers, in the end, that 'not only does the sense of *the other* as such never appear in Moreri and his readers, but on the contrary, by means of colonialism, the dream is merging into reality: the dream of making the whole earth co-extensive with *us* (*chez nous*), and thus unifying the globe under the banner of Christian Europe'.[35]

Two views of primitive man continued to exist side by side, as they were to be found in José de Acosta. He was seen either as a brutish, cruel, fierce, wild barbarian,[36] or as an innocent, mild, docile, gentle savage, of good disposition, virtuous, happy.[37] In the eighteenth century, to provide ideological backing for a triumphant bourgeoisie, Rousseau was to present the *bon sauvage* as distinct from the 'natural state' and the 'civil state' (or feudal, monarchical, medieval civilisation). Thus he said that 'we must take care neither to confuse the natural state with the savage state (*l'état sauvage*), nor, on the other hand, the natural state with the civil state (*l'état civil*).[38] The *bon sauvage* (or primitive man with positive characteristics—as in the first and second of de Acosta's categories, or the second of the two types mentioned above) stands as a criticism of the 'civil state', or feudal, monarchical culture. In fact the 'state of nature' is that of the bourgeois subject emerging in a pure and free condition in order to create a new world (capitalist Europe from the eighteenth century onwards).[39] In this case the *bon sauvage* is the positive view the triumphant bourgeoisie takes of the peoples of the Third World as possible subjects for exploitation, now secularised (the question is no longer whether they can receive the faith, as with the rough (*rudos*) Indians of the Spanish conquest; nor yet whether they are disbelieving pagans as seen by French Christianity in the seventeenth century), and thus available as cheap manpower or as possible markets for its industrial merchandise: 'Such a (bourgeois) society is led to seek new consumers, outside itself, and so it will seek means of subsisting among other peoples who are its inferiors in the matter of the resources of which it has a superfluity, or in terms of industry in general.'[40]

The countries of the Third World, who represent the *bon sauvage*, are thus considered as a *tabula rasa*, an extra and cheap productive force, a potential market for over-production, the *raw material* of civilisation. The great 'theologian' of Europe's domination in the world actually says in his 'modern' *Summa theologiae*: 'The material existence of England is based on trade (*Handel*) and industry (*Industrie*), and the English have accepted for themselves the role of *missionaries* (*die Missionarien*; notice the religious connotation) of *civilisation* throughout the world. Thus their commercial spirit (*Handelsgeist*, the Holy Spirit of capitalism?) impels them to explore all seas and all lands, to make alliances with barbarian peoples (*barbarischen Völkern*), to arouse in them new needs and industries, and, above all, to create in them the conditions necessary for engaging in human relations, that is, the renunciation of acts of violence, respect for poverty(!) and 'hospitality' (towards capital, Hegel forgot to add!).[41]

We Latin Americans, the first 'barbarians' of Europe's Modern Age—the Africans and Asians were to follow us in due course—have been acquainted with this 'theology' for five centuries, but in our time it has become more tragic. The actual number of *rudos*, noble savages, barbarians, is today the number of 'underdeveloped countries', countries of the Third World, poor countries.

This *civil religion* is, as ever, the ideological justification which salves the conscience of capitalism as it exploits the new *rudos, sauvages*, barbarians: the peoples of the Third World. Moreover, the difference between worthy (*dignos*) 'men' and unworthy (*indignos*) 'barbarians' is said to have its origin in the 'divine plan' or in 'nature': 'Disparities in conditions between political entities are natural.'[42]

How far removed we are from that Christian doctrine which Peter taught Cornelius, the pagan, the barbarian, one of the *goim*:

> Stand up; I too am a man (*autos anthrōpos*). . . . Truly I perceive that God shows no partiality (*ouk estin prosopolēmptēs*), but in any nation anyone who fears him and does what is right (*dikaiosynēn*) is acceptance to him (Acts 10:26, 34-35).

Translated by G. W. S. Knowles

Notes

1. *Obras del padre José de Acosta* (BAE Madrid 1954) p. 392a.
2. The author bases himself on Thomas *In Epist. ad Rom.*, c.l., lect. 5; and *I ad Cor.*, c. 14, lect. 2.
3. J. de Acosta *De procuranda*.
4. *Op. cit.* p. 392b.
5. *Loc. cit.*
6. *Loc. cit.*
7. *Ibid.* p. 393b.
8. *Conquête et exploitation des nouveaux mondes* (PUF Paris 1969) p. 7.
9. *Op. cit.* (BAE Madrid 1959) III p. 60. See Lewis Hanke *Uno es el género humano* (Chiapas 1974) pp. 54 ff.
10. *Democrates Alter* (CSIC Madrid 1957) p. 15.
11. See Kittel *TWNT* II pp. 362 ff, art. 'ethnos'.
12. 'Exteriority' (Aüsserlichkeit) is for Hegel 'existence' (*Dasein*): what is farthest removed from 'being' (springing originally from the division

(*Entzweiung*) of being). For us (see *Filosofía ética latinoamericana* [Edicol Mexico 1977]) 'exteriority' is the sphere from which *the other*, the poor insofar as he is unconditioned by the oppressing system and *outside* our world, demands justice.

13. 'Mobilisation against the Enemy acts as a powerful impulse to production and employment, and thus maintains a high standard of living. . . . The alienation of the totality absorbs particular alienations and converts crimes against humanity into a rational undertaking' (H. Marcuse *One Dimensional Man*, 2 [Spanish edition Mortiz, Mexico 1969] pp. 43 and 73).

14. In the preaching of Jesus as a whole we observe an openness to the one who is 'other than' the Jewish people. See J. Jeremias *Jésus et les paiens* (Neuchâtel, Delachaux, 1956).

15. Kittel *TWNT* V p. 453.

16. Lewis Hanke *Uno es* p. 9.

17. *Pol.* I 5 1254a 14-16, 1254b 19-24.

18. *Sobre las justas causas de la guerra contra los indios* (Fondo de Cultura Económica, Mexico 1941) p. 81.

19. Stafford Poole *Bartolomé de las Casas. Defense against the Persecutors and Slanderers for the People of the New World* (De Kalb, Illinois 1974) p. 333.

20. *Ibid.* p. 338.

21. *Ibid.* p. 329.

22. The 'blinded eyes' are precisely the *blind* ethical conscience (*Gewissen*), D. von Hildebrand would say. See his *Die Idee der sittlichen Handlung* (Damstadt 1969).

23. S. Poole *Bartolomé de las Casas* pp. 345-346.

24. *Ibid.* p. 353.

25. *Brevísma relación de la destrucción de las Indias* (BAE Madrid) V p. 136a.

26. *Historia de las Indias* I ch. 40 p. 142a.

27. This is how Hobbes defined European man, the product of bourgeois capitalism: '*Homo homini lupus*'.

28. *Brevísima relación* p. 136b.

29. *Historia de las Indias* III ch. 79 II p. 357a.

30. *Representación a los regentes Cisneros y Adriano* V p. 3a.

31. *Memorial de remedios* V p. 120a.

32. *Cláusula del testamento* V p. 540a.

33. *Cláusula del testamento* V p. 540a, b.

34. Article 'Europe' in the *Grand dictionnaire historique* ed. L. Moreri (Provence 1643). See Bernard Duchene 'Un exemple d'univers mental au XVIIIe. siècle' in *Civilisation chrétienne* (Paris) pp. 29-30.

35. *Ibid.* p. 44.

36. *Ibid.* p. 35.

37. *Loc. cit.*

38. *Emile ou de l'éducation* (Paris 1964) p. 514.

39. See my work *Ética filosófica latinoamericana* (Mexico 1977) III pp. 136 ff.

40. Hegel *Rechtsphilosophie* p. 246.

41. *Idem. Philosophie der Geschichte* (Frankfurt 1970) XII p. 538.

42. R. Cooper, K. Kaiser and M. Kosaka *Towards a Renovated International System* (1977) (typewritten text of the Trilateral Commission) p. 21.

Part III

Present Christian Practice of 'Neither Jew nor Greek, neither slave nor free, neither male or female'

Leonidas E. Proaño

The Church and the Poor
in Latin America Today

INTRODUCTION

THE CHURCH and the poor in Latin America today is a subject of crucial importance to the Church itself as well as to the poor in Latin America.

It is important to the Church because it is concerned with how the Church regards the poor, and itself in relation to the poor, how far it is faithful to Christ's teaching about poverty and siding with the poor, today, in the huge area known as Latin America. Basically this is a test of authenticity and faithfulness to Christ, because the Church is called to become and to be a continuation of Christ in space and time, to complete, through the Spirit, his mission of salvation.

It is important to the poor because it seeks to discover whether the Church can kindle any light in their darkness to give them a ray of hope. We need to know how the poor see the Church and themselves in relation to it, how far they feel themselves to be active members of the Church, the people of God. We want to know whether the poor feel called, through the Church to identify with Christ, because he first identified with them, and thus to realise that they are the ones who are called to become and be the Church. They are privileged to proclaim the gospel to the world, because they are fitter then anyone else to proclaim by word and action that the kingdom of God is near.

First we must describe who are the poor in Latin America, their place in society, what they do, say, want and hope (1).

Then I shall try to describe the various attitudes of the Church in relation to the poor (2).

Thirdly I examine the Church's authenticity in the light of the gospel (3).

1. *Who are they?*

When we speak of the poor, many people object to the term by saying that the rich are also poor. Here we have no need to discuss the fact that all people, whatever their socio-economic position, are poor because we are all limited creatures and sinners. Here when we speak of the poor we mean the many men and women in Latin America who lack material necessities, are oppressed by the social structure, are not cared for by the services of the state and are unable to better their own situation or take part in decision-making.

In Latin America the poor are the Indians, the negroes, the peasants, the slum-dwellers, the unemployed or under-employed, the workers and many skilled craftsmen. If we imagine the structure of society as a pyramid, the poor are the people at its base, who suffer the full weight of domination by social classes above them, and are despised.

2. *What do they do?*

Some of the poor work, either on the land or in the city. They work the land for people who call themselves landowners. Nowadays landowners are often large agricultural companies, which are sometimes multi-national. Some of the poor work themselves to death building roads, or enormous buildings or luxury houses. Some of the poor work as loaders in the cities, especially in the Andean countries, or as dockers in the ports. Some work at humble crafts and are badly paid and exploited by middle men. Some work in factories in inhuman conditions for low wages. Some work in the mines without due protective measures for their life and health. Some cannot find work and do odd jobs to survive in constant anxiety and uncertainty. For this reason many of them turn to robbery, pillage and vice.

3. *What do they say?*

In Latin America some of the poor say nothing and some have regained the power to speak. The former are the 'voiceless', they belong to the 'culture of silence'; they are oppressed and have been for centuries and are in the grip of a mass of prejudices, superstitions, compulsions and inhibitions, fantasies, fatalism, conformism, hopelessness and passivity (*Educacion* 3, Medellin).

The latter are those who have awakened such people from their centuries-old lethargy and have reached a stage of self-awareness enabling them to speak, to start becoming human again and voice their complaint, their demand for justice and their aspirations. These were the poor referred to by the bishops at Medellin when they spoke of a 'growing awareness among the oppressed' (*Paz* 7) and said that 'a murmur is arising from millions of people asking their shepherds for a freedom which never comes' (*Pobreza* 2). And these were the people the bishops at Puebla meant when they compared the situation today to that of ten years ago, saying: 'From the heart of the different countries that make up Latin America an ever more insistent and turbulent cry is rising to heaven', adding that now this cry is no longer a murmur but 'clear, growing louder, more impetuous and sometimes threatening.' (*Vision de lar realidad eclesial hoy in America Latina* pp. 87 and 89.)

4. *What do they want?*

The poor who have attained some self-awareness urgently seek liberation from their inhuman living conditions, from exploitation and oppression, from lives used to work for the enrichment of the few. They seek lives which are more human, in which justice reigns and the person counts, the power to take part in decision-making.

In order to achieve this, they feel the need to organise themselves, to unite in solidarity with their suffering brothers, and fight tirelessly for the creation of a new, more just and human society.

5. *What do they hope?*

They have been repeatedly disappointed by demagogic politicians who gave them all sorts of promises merely from the desire to catch their votes and who then forgot all about their promises and left them in the same miserable state they were in before. Lately dictatorships and military governments have viciously suppressed the demands of the poor for justice and their attempts at organisation. Who can they turn to?

Most of the poor in Latin America still turn to the Church with hope and confidence. When the pope visited Mexico and the Episcopal Conference was being held at Puebla, the poor of Mexico wrote a letter to the pope saying: 'With any luck this time you will rouse us and we will wake up at last. This is why we will come to see you. We will expect you in the Guadalupe villa where we always go when something is worrying us a lot.' Referring to the Conference they said, '. . . we need this meeting to give us strong support like that other one in which they said that the people need to free themselves.' (*Vida Nueva* 1.176, p. 5.)

2. THE CHURCH IN LATIN AMERICA TODAY

What is the attitude of the Church towards the poor in Latin America today? The bishops at Puebla in their *Opcion preferencial por los pobres* give us their answer to this question. They say: 'Not all of us in the Church in Latin America have become involved enough with the poor. We do not always care about them and side with them.' (1.140.)

If we look at the Church as a whole in Latin America, we can say that it takes two contradictory stances. There is the rich Church allied to the powerful, and the poor Church which is involved with the poor.

1. *Rich and allied to the powerful*

One side of the Church is conservative and accumulates material goods, honours, privileges, connections with those who hold economic, political and social power. This may take the form of looking backwards to the past with obstinate conservatism or looking to the present which has emerged from the past and siding with modernisation and development. These two positions are basically the same. However, siding with modernisation and development is more dangerous because it is supported by spurious justifications which quieten the conscience and quieten the poor themselves, but is still devoted to the maintenance of the status quo. When the Church takes this attitude the poor hardly count, they are treated as inferior beings, children who need to be led by the hand and mothered. Authority descends from the top and there is no room for the voice of the poor. This is the Church favoured by governments who follow an ideology of National Security. This Church collaborates efficiently in keeping the people under, as a silent, passive, harmless and impersonal mass.

This attitude sees order as something 'sacred' and untouchable, peace as something which must not be disturbed either by words or actions which demand justice, because this peace is identified with the 'established order'. This attitude, especially when it goes together with an urge to modernise, supports a model of development imported from rich countries, forgetting that the rich countries are rich at the expense of the poor countries. On this basis, by education the Church means the training of economically privileged young people and adults to maintain and administer a society in which there are oppressors and oppressed, rich and poor; while for the common people 'education' is a conditioning process to make them accept this state of affairs. With this attitude, the Church thinks of imposing the faith as a body of dogmas that must be believed, a body of religious and pious practices which must be gone through to save your soul. Popular religiosity is encouraged indiscriminately and the Church refuses to encourage a faith understood as a commitment to Christ's transforming mission. With this attitude, the Church distrusts popular organisations and is hostile to them to the point of excommunicating those who have taken part in them without its consent.

The poor also have an attitude to this conservative and modernising Church. They see it as alien from them, an institution much like other institutions from which certain religious services are sometimes required. They do not feel they are members of it. They are afraid of it because it is powerful and allied to the powerful. They cannot discover Christ in it, Christ who was poor and a friend of the poor. Although they have submitted to this Church up till now, they are finally beginning turn away and leave it.

2. *Poor and involved with the poor*

The reply to the question 'What is the Church in Latin America's attitude to the poor today?' is given in the same text from Puebla. Although the whole Church in Latin America has not identified properly with the poor, we can say that many of us *have* identified with them. This is the other side of the coin: a Church which is poor and involved with the poor because it is made up of the poor.

In Medellin, this Church began by making a public confession: 'In this context of poverty and even misery in which the great majority of Latin American people live, we bishops, priests and religious have the necessities of life and a certain security, whereas the poor lack indispensable necessities and live in fear and uncertainty. There is no lack of cases in which the poor feel that their bishops, parish priests and religious do not really identify with them, with their problems and fears, do not always support those who work with them or care about their fate.' (*Pobreza de la Iglesia* 3, Medellin).

As a result of this confession of guilt, some members of the Church in Latin America began to turn towards poverty and increasing involvement with the poor. The bishops at Puebla recognised it plainly: 'We found that national episcopates and many groups of layfolk, monks, nuns and priests were becoming more deeply and genuinely involved with the poor. This new but real witness led the Latin American Church to denounce the grave injustices caused by oppressive structures.' (*Opcion Preferencial por los Pobres,* 1136.) Thus the Puebla Conference in its document 'Vita Consagrada' encouraged religious to follow this way: 'Encourage religious to take sides with the poor.' This was after agreeing that this 'siding', this 'priority choice of the poor was the most important tendency in Latin American religious life'. The document stressed the fact that 'more and more frequently religious work in poor and deprived areas, missions to the destitute, in patient and humble work'. (769 and 733.)

Having noted and qoted official documents of the Latin American Church on this choice and involvement with the poor, we must now say something about the consequences of this attitude for many members of the Church. Many lay people, nuns, monks and priests have suffered because they have taken sides with the poor and fought for justice. Although we need to inquire into the motives of these numerous Christians who have taken sides with the poor, even at the risk of their lives, there is no doubt at all that very many of them were motivated by faith. With this attitude, the Church sees the poor as the Lord's favourites, the real bearers of the gospel to a world overwhelmed by materialism and injustice, the most able to receive the 'good news of the kingdom', and to live by it and bear witness to it before the world.

For their part, the authorities who support the ideology and laws of National Security, regard people with this vision of the Church not only just with distrust but with aggressive hostility. They have unleashed a whole terror of refined persecutions. They have cleverly avoided attacking the Church as such but managed to separate particular members of the Church so that they could discredit them and thus were free to bring about their moral or physical destruction. These particular members of the Church were precisely those who had chosen to side with the poor.

Puebla recognised these facts: 'The Church's prophetic denunciation of injustice and real involvement with the poor brought upon it in many cases persecution and other troubles. The poor themselves were the first victims.' (*Opcion Preferencial por los pobres* 1138.)

The poor too expressed their opinion on the Church's involvement with them. From many witnesses we choose the following to quote: 'The poor feel they are genuine members of the Church and share directly in the decision taken to bring about social and religious improvement. The Church is weaning people from popular religiosity and leading them to a more authentic and solid life of faith, creating a feeling of solidarity with those who suffer for justice' sake.' (Reply of a group of Christian people to the question: 'What changes of attitude can be seen in the Church in its relationship with the poor?' Christian Lenten Assemblies, Riobamba 1979.) Thus the poor feel they are members of the Church.

3. AUTHENTICITY OF THE CHURCH

The Church has a duty to strive for identification with Christ. It is a duty of faithfulness so that the Church can be called and be the Church of Christ. This striving for identification with Christ must take account of all his characteristics. Among them the Church must make every effort to identify with Christ is his relationship to poverty and the poor. It is most important to examine the identity of the Church in Latin America in order to strive constantly for its conversion. Such an examination could also be very useful to the churches in other places, starting with Europe, so that they too may strive for conversion.

1. *Christ and poverty*

It is quite clear and irrefutable that Christ took on poverty. Christ became poor not only in the sense that he took on the poverty of the human condition in general, but above all in the sense that he took on the poverty of the poor: he became poor among the poor. He was born into a poor family. He was born in extreme poverty; his mother 'laid him in a manger because there was no room at the inn'. He grew up in poverty. He worked as a poor man. For the proclamation of 'the good news' he used poor means. His supreme act of poverty was to surrender his life between two thieves. The very fact of choosing the Jewish people to make his own was a proof of poverty because they were a small, insignificant country subjugated by Rome; if he had been born in Rome he would have been another sort of man, just as nowadays people who are born as citizens of rich countries, which are the real empires today, are different from people who are born in Third World countries which are kindly described as 'developing'.

Face to face with Christ the poor man, Christ who is the mirror in which the Church must look at itself, what is the Church like in Latin America today? Is it really poor? Which of the two positions we described above succeeds in identifying with the Son of God made man?

Christ did not only become poor among the poor but he also confronted the rich. As a poor man he condemned wealth and said that God did not choose the rich: 'It is impossible to serve God and Mammon.' (Matt. 6:24.)

2. *From among the poor*

Christ became poor. In spite of this Christ could have chosen rich people to form his Church. But he did not; he chose the poor. Most of his disciples were fishermen, who are poor and uneducated people anywhere in the world. And if any of them were not poor, their calling by Christ impelled them to become poor. Just as it is unquestionable that Christ became poor, it is also unquestionable that he chose to form his Church from among the poor. And from among the poor he chose to exercise his mission to save the world and bring the kingdom of the Father. When he had chosen poor people to be his disciples and apostles, he preached his message: 'Blessed are the poor . . .' and showed kindness and compassion to the multitude of hungry, sick and sinners. . . . He demonstrated His practical solidarity with the poor. And on the other hand He condemned the rich fiercely.

Which position of the Church in Latin America is closest to Christ? Which of the two very distinct positions of the Church in Latin America is a closer identification with Christ who was poor and a brother to the poor? . . .

Let us hope that soon the Church in Latin America, formed from the poor, may be able to reply as Christ did to the questions of John the Baptist: "Go and tell John what you have seen and heard: the blind receive their sight, the lame walk, lepers are cleansed, and the deaf hear, the dead are raised up, the poor have 'the good news' preached to them." (Luke 7:22.)

Translated by Dinah Livingstone

Donna Singles

The Case of Women
in the Church:
Objection Sustained

THE fact cannot be denied: solely because of their sex, women are rigorously excluded from all responsibilities in the teaching, governing and sacramental Church which suppose ordination as a prerequisite. Certainly one cannot deny that women now have a far greater place in the Church community than in the past—especially since the Second Vatican Council. But in no way does this change the principle which excludes women from all ministries demanding *a priori* ordination. The present legislation of the Church simply reflects this principle: the feminine sex constitutes a formal *impedimentum* against the admission of women to Holy Orders. Thus, before all other considerations and in an unequivocal manner, women are eliminated from certain vital sectors of Church life for no other reason than their sex. This should not be taken to mean, of course, that ministries in the Church open to women are unimportant or demeaning. They are simply and always subordinate to hierarchical functions in the ecclesiastical community.

Does it follow that women are minors in the Church? That their exclusion from public ecclesial office gives them an inferior status? Does it constitute a real affront to their dignity? A non-evangelical form of discrimination?

Such questions preoccupy the growing number of Christians who are coming to think that fidelity to the gospel demands a change in the Church's present practice with regard to women. They find it increasingly difficult to understand why the Church remains paralysed by traditional views of women while changes in all other sectors of society are creating

new relationships between men and women as well as a new understanding of the feminine person. Must one conclude from this that Church
authorities continue to preach a classical image of woman because they
consider it a divinely revealed concept? Or do they cling to it out of fear
that another image would entail such far-reaching changes in the liturgy
and in the teaching and governing offices, that it is better to maintain the
traditional view of woman? Ultimately, what is at stake here is more than
the question of man-woman relationships in the Christian community; it
is a question of the nature of the Church herself. The official stance she
has taken in our times toward women is seen by many as a denial of her
own vocation to move unceasingly toward conversion.[1]

One wonders if it is possible for the Church to maintain her credibility
if, at the same time that she insists on the dignity of man in the name of the
gospel, she refrains from seriously criticising her own image of woman—
an image which unfortunately continues to dictate her objections to
women's entry into vital areas of Church life. One can also wonder how
effective the Church's denunciation of discrimination can be[2] while she
continues to justify the existence of a sacramental and governmental
system entirely in the hands of men.

Thus, the present debate on the place of women in the Church touches
the problem of what she is in herself. As long as the ecclesial institution
continues to reason in terms of the traditional image of woman, it will see
no reason to question either its attitude toward women or its concept of
Orders as an exclusively masculine structure.

This, it seems, is where the real problem lies. However, rather than
grapple with it directly—an approach hardly realistic in the brief space of
an article—I prefer to limit myself to the single question of *meaning*.
What sense can be made of woman's exclusion from vital functions of
Church life? Of the fact that a particular image of woman continues to
dictate this exclusion? Indeed, the most urgent task at the moment is to
bring that image out into the open, especially as it is conveyed by documents and statements of the institutional Church, and to show how it
functions as an effective obstacle to woman's full participation in the
Christian community. This is the sense of the two examples proposed
below, one taken from the Church's official theory, the other from a
practical application of this theory.

1. REPRESENTATION REQUIRES RESEMBLANCE

The first of the two examples is taken from the commentary which
accompanied the publication of the document *Inter Insigniores* by the
Congregation of the Faith on January 28 1977. The curial text stated that
'The Church, in fidelity to the example of the Lord, does not consider

herself authorised to admit women to priestly ordination'.[3] The author of the accompanying commentary—who remains anonymous—tries to clarify the Roman decision for those who intellectually find passive and blind obedience impossible. At the same time, however, the author adds that the Church's magisterium concerns the decision itself rather than any explanation which would seek to justify it.[4] Toward the end of his exposé, the author evokes the difficult question of representation: Is it possible for a woman to represent Christ in acts essential to the New Covenant? He replies that in the exercise of those acts which require the sacerdotal character, the priest is a sign of Christ and must therefore be a man.

'Natural resemblance' between the Saviour and the one who signifies him is the condition *sine qua non* for the exercise of a function carried out 'in the name and in the place of Christ'.[5] Wishing to give his argument theological support, the author continues: '. . . the fact that Christ is a man and not a woman is neither accidental nor unimportant . . . since the economy of salvation has been revealed by symbols essential to it, without which God's plan would remain unintelligible for us.'[6]

In the same manner we are told that the Old Testament, formulated in terms of a marriage covenant, and the New Testament in those of a nuptial contract between Christ and his Church, explain why the masculine sex is absolutely required in those situations where a human being is called upon to 'assume the role of Christ, to be a sign of his presence, that is, to represent him—in other words, to be an efficacious sign of his presence in the essential acts of the covenant'.[7] The author of the commentary ends his demonstration with an all-encompassing affirmation: to question the biblical symbol of the marriage covenant is 'to question the very status of Revelation, it is to reject the value of Scripture'.[8] As a follow-up to this massive statement, the author adds: 'It is perhaps even more a profound ignorance of the human value of the nuptial theme in the revelation of God's love.'[9]

Doubtless, we are at the heart of the argument to which those opposed to women's ordination appeal. One may well ask oneself, however, what happens when the argument is examined more closely. It is quite possible that the idealisation of the masculine sex equally implies an ideal of woman which even a rapid analysis would find fundamentally ambiguous.

With this in mind, let us come back to the demonstration proposed by the commentary of *Inter Insigniores*. Essentially, the author's argument can be stated as follows: The priest, by assuming the *role* of Christ, becomes at the same time an efficacious *sign* of his presence as well as his *representative* thanks to the natural *resemblance* which the masculine sex accords him—this latter being considered an indispensable aspect of all biblical *symbols* related to the theme of Christ-spouse.

In spite of the obvious confusion here between different planes of reasoning (due to the fact that sexual resemblance is here considered essential to both the roles of representation and signification), the argument itself evokes for us the idea deduced from Tridentine theology that the character of ordination 'configures' the priest to Christ. It should be remembered, however, that in the sixteenth century, the council fathers were reacting to the Protestants when they placed the accent on the sacramental and sacerdotal aspects of Orders. It was not their intention to offer a complete definition of the sacrament. The model of the priesthood which they proposed was partial, centred upon the notion of the sacerdotal character.

Evidently, such a model, translated into ontological categories would mean a configuration to Christ more concerned with the priest's *being* than with the *functions* which he assures in the Christian community. This is why such a model can easily become a sort of trap, leading those who invoke it dangerously close to the impossible theological position which holds that the priest should be defined by analogy with the Incarnation. Yet, this is precisely the idea which the author of the commentary seems to be proposing when he affirms that 'natural resemblance', an indispensable support of the faith, is necessary for a correct understanding of the link between the symbolic language of the covenant and the assimilation of the priest to the person of Christ.

Obviously, such an image of the priest's role presents a grave difficulty insofar as it tends to immobolise in the form of absolute categories the semantic qualities which characterise it. In fact, this is the very difficulty inherent in the classic theology of Orders. This becomes particularly evident when one sees that its development over the centuries followed to a great extent the natural bent of the imagination (which, for the Christian, creates an incredibly strong and profound link between priesthood and masculinity). One understands better why the image of the priest that resulted from this development was unable to integrate women into its perspectives. The idea which prevailed in the beginning grew out of the need of the Christian community to signify the distance between itself and Christ: the Church does not exist in and for herself; she is not her own source of salvation.

These ideas, the Church found, could best be expressed by the notion of representation. The priest, called upon to signify Christ's *vis-à-vis* with the community of believers, thus came to be thought of as representing the distance between man and divine graciousness. As the concept evolved, it tended to narrow the distance between the priest and Christ: starting with the idea that he acts in the Lord's name, one came to think of the priest as taking, in fact, his place. Thus the theology of priesthood gradually established a rupture between the community and its ordained minister while, at the same time, seeing an ever greater link between the latter and the person of Christ. The result of this process could be foreseen: the priest and Christ are considered as one. The ordained minister becomes another Christ, an '*alter Christus*'.[10]

In the light of such thinking, it is not surprising that the notion of 'natural resemblance', in the form of phantasm, should enter the picture. Thanks to its particularly effective power of evocation, the notion of similitude was pushed to the extreme: the image gives me reality; when I see the priest, I am seeing Christ. Thus, the classic concept of priesthood follows the logic of the imagination—the latter retaining, evidently, the quality of masculinity as a necessary characteristic of Christ's image.[11]

Obviously, the symbolism of the priest as sign of Christ's otherness *vis-à-vis* the Church is quite lost in a process born of the nostalgic need to render Christ present through the agency of a human being having in common with the historical Jesus the quality of masculinity. Does such a conception of priesthood also imply something about women? One thing, at least: their marginalisation in the Church will continue as long as religious imagination identifies the priest with the historical Christ and theologians consider natural resemblance a necessary condition for a correct understanding of the role of the ordained minister. Where sexual differentiation is maintained as an essential criterion of the relationship between Christ and the ordained minister, womanhood and priesthood will continue to be mutually exclusive values. To the extent that official Church language proposes an image of the priest bordering on phantasm, to the extent that representation is confused with similitude, it seems wishful thinking to hope for the ordination of women. It should be evident that insistance on the masculine sex as a necessary means of understanding the symbolical role of representation is also an effective way of excluding women from this role. But it is also a doubtful understanding of divine Revelation: such an approach gives the impression, wrongly, that the tendency of the imagination to accent the importance of one signifier to the detriment of others is in conformity with the faith. Such a tendency explains why a particular effort of lucidity is required of the believer in his interpretation of religious symbols. Care must ever be taken not to confuse divine Revelation with the relativity of the language through which it is expressed. Only in this way can it be hoped that the masculine sex will cease to be considered as a necessary criterion in the choice of the Church's ministers.

2. TRADITION ADMITS ONLY THE MASCULINE SEX

Turning to another example should help to show that not only the theory of the institutional Church has an ambiguous attitude toward women; the same can also be seen in practical areas of her life where no question of ordination or resemblance to Christ is at stake. Among women who work closely with the Church—religious, catechists, parish helpers, etc.—few have never experienced difficulty with the institution on account of their sex. There are instances where no canon or other Church regulation can be cited to explain the reticence of the clergy to allow woman to occupy positions of responsibility. On occasion, the embarrassment of authorities is particularly evident in their inability to offer convincing and reasonable arguments for this reticence. One incident which comes to mind—while somewhat dated and of minor importance for the world of Church diplomacy—may serve as an example.

In December, 1969, the nomination of Mrs Elisabeth Müller as adviser to the German ambassador of the Holy See met with a negative response on the part of the Vatican Secretary of State. In spite of efforts to justify their disapproval, Roman authorities betrayed a certain discomfort in their declaration to the public: 'Tradition wishes that representatives to the Vatican be of the masculine sex.'[12] As adviser to the diplomatic corps to the Holy See, Mrs Müller would have had to assure the role of *chargé d'affaires* in the absence of the ambassador—a role which would have put her in direct contact with ecclesiastical dignitaries at the highest level of negotiations. Such a possibility, however, was not acceptable to the Vatican.

The incident is revealing. By placing the question of women on a level of argument where there is no question of ordination, one sees that her marginalisation in the Church cannot be reduced to purely theological grounds. Women's exclusion from vital centres of Church activity must be attributed rather to the long history which considered woman as subordinate to man—a history in which the case of Mrs Müller finds its rightful place. The unfavourable reply of the Vatican raises the further question of a totally masculine hierarchy. More specifically still, it raises a fundamental problem illustrated by the following points:

> *Tradition* does not accept the presence of women at the highest levels of decision-making in the Church;
> Woman is not called upon to exercise *authority* in the Church to the same extent as men;
> The *public* character of high posts of responsibility in the Vatican make the appointment of women to these offices undesirable;
> Such appointments are all the more unacceptable in that they are likely to bring women into *direct contact with an entirely male, celibate body of men*.

Such are the conclusions that can be drawn from Rome's decision in the 'Müller affair'. The institution's negative reply thus leads one to look beyond purely objective arguments in order to understand why Church authorities persist in the practice of reserving the sacramental, teaching and governing functions to men. It would seem, in fact, that the roles of the imagination and of the emotions should be examined as a possible source of such attitudes.

Without going further than the case of Mrs Müller, one might well conclude that there is something about a woman's presence that renders the clergy uneasy. It is true that difference is a problem for the person who has yet to come to terms with his own identity. Might this explain why the Holy See did not wish to see a woman in 'direct contact' with Church dignitaries?

The idea comes all the more spontaneously to mind by reason of the fact that the post for which Mrs Müller was selected could have put her in situations where she would have had to exercise authority in an official and public capacity.

It is well-known that sexual anxieties of prudishness nourished by phantasms arising from the incapacity to cope with difference are not incompatible with the desire for power. The contrary is often the case. In order to overcome the threat of what is unfamiliar or dissimilar, the other is dominated, subordinated, treated with aversion. A less evident but no less important form of this attitude can be found in the idea that 'nature' determines the roles and functions of individuals. It is thus that the Church has long appealed to the notion of complementarity of the sexes in order to justify her relegation of women to the private tasks of wife and mother. As for man's exercise of power in the Church, its *raison d'être* has been found in the incarnation of God as man. This is perfectly in line with the lesson of the Roman document *Inter Insigniores* that Christ delegated his authority and his power solely to men. Yet, nothing prevents the imagination from entering quietly upon the scene in support of such reasoning: the ancient images of man—centre of the world, the Son, the Father—are not, in fact, foreign to the idea of man in the image of the fatherhood of God.

Should one conclude from this that these fears and desire for power played a part in the Holy See's unfavourable answer to the German embassy? It is impossible to make such an affirmation with certitude since we are dealing here with twilight zones of consciousness; yet one cannot prevent the suspicion from suggesting itself in view of the appeal of the Roman authorities to tradition. The weakness of their argument is obvious: no tradition, in fact, exists which forbids women to become members of the Holy See's diplomatic corps since the question has never arisen.[13]

One is thus led to think that in this matter as in that of ordination, the marginalisation of half of the Church's baptised population is due to reasons other than fidelity to the gospel of Jesus Christ. Certainly, one does not ask the institution to change radically its practice immediately and without preparation. But it could begin even now by refusing to let itself be blinded by unwarranted motives which have inspired its past attitude toward women and by submitting these same motives to rigorous and objective examination. This would surely be an important step toward the construction of a more credible Church in the eyes of our contemporaries. It would also be the best way to prepare the Christian community for the future when women will fully participate at all levels of Church life.

As stated earlier, I have made no effort here to exhaust the subject. On the contrary, it deserves much more extensive and subtle development. In conclusion, my hope is simply that the two examples cited in these pages will serve to show that a real problem exists and that it demands of the Church—in theory and practice—a thorough re-evaluation of her discourse, a courageous overcoming of her fears and an actualisation of her traditions that she might answer the new needs of our time in full collaboration with women.

Notes

1. See *Lumen Gentium* 1:8.

2. See *Glaudium et Spes* Part 1, Ch. 2.

3. *Declaration on the Question of Admission of Women to the Ministerial Priesthood* (London 1976) p. 5.

4. 'Commentary on the Declaration of the Congregation of the Faith concerning the Question of the Admission of Women to the Ministerial Priesthood in *La Documentation Catholique*, cited hereafter as *D.C.*

5. *D.C.* p. 172.

6. *D.C.* pp. 172-173.

7. *D.C.* p. 173.

8. *D.C.* p. 173.

9. *Ibid.*

10. It should be noted here that even the French school of spirituality which so much insisted on resemblance between the priest and Christ did not go as far as the Roman document. For Olier and his followers, resemblance to Christ was to be seen in the priest's *holiness*, not in his *physical* similarity to the Saviour. 'We are his [Christ's] image at the altar . . . but we do not resemble him except to the extent that we unceasingly force ourselves to become exactly like him in our lives, in the holiness of our actions.'—P. Metezeau *De Sancto Sacerdotio* (Paris 1631) pp. 99-100, cited by I. Noye 'Sacerdoce et sainteté' in *La Tradition sacerdotale* ed. X. Mappus (1959) p. 185 (E.T. supplied).

11. One does not ask that the imagination do what it cannot do, that is abandon its image of Christ as man. The problem is rather to *situate Christ's masculinity correctly vis-à-vis* priestly functions and to recall other neglected or forgotten aspects of this function. The idea, for example, that the *entire community* acts in and through Christ is absent from the classic image of the priest. Yet, the advantage of this theology is obvious in that it implies an ordained ministry without *a priori* links to masculinity.

12. What is given here is my translation of the Vatican's statement as it was communicated by a notice of Agence France-Presse, 25th January 1970.

13. It is true that the Holy See accorded full diplomatic recognition to a secretary of the Dutch embassy, Miss Bartelds, but her rank did not imply dealing on official level with high Vatican dignitaries. As for Mrs Clare Booth Luce, U.S. ambassador during the reign of Pius XII, her responsibility was directly to the Quirinal; no U.S. embassy to the Vatican exists.

Francisco F. Claver

Christian Communities in Regard Ethnic or Tribal Minorities

1. THE PROBLEM

IN the general rhetoric on human rights—a current, almost faddish, issue these days—the rights of minorities come in for plenty of discussion and dissection. But often, in all the talk, the minorities themselves are, by some strange oversight, left out from the actual conversation. This fact is possibly the ultimate indignity done to those without dignity, unintended but perpetrated nonetheless by well-meaning people, themselves concerned with restoring lost dignity to others. The irony could well stem from the very idea of 'restoring' other people's dignity.

It is a main presupposition of this paper that human dignity, like the rights that flow from it, is inalienable and, if we are to be precise, cannot be 'lost' or 'restored'. Perhaps this is quibbling. But the fact is, if human dignity is indeed inalienable, one person cannot restore it to another. And from this a further and most pragmatic deduction is that human dignity is best validated when it is asserted by the very people who are thought to be without it. And if all this is true, it is a gospel task of the first order for Christians to abet that act of asserting dignity. Thus, if we must talk of 'restoring' dignity, we would do well to do so in terms of its deliberate asserting.

In the light of all this, the problem of human dignity *vis-à-vis* professedly Christian communities and *their* relations with ethnic minorities becomes a fertile spawning ground for further questions. For the depressingly uniform fact seems to be that when Christians pride themselves on being God's chosen race—the 'prejudice of the *Saved*'—all others become by that very fact of lesser status as human beings. The trait is not, probably, a specifically Christian failing but occurs whenever a people sets itself apart as superior to others for whatever reason—skin-colour, diet, clothing, ideology, religion, etc. But for Christians who profess as part of their belief the common dignity of all men and women under the Fatherhood of God, the question becomes, or should become, not merely one of human prejudice but of religion as well, a question that strikes deep into the very foundations of Christianity itself: 'If you did this to the least of my brethren. . . .'

But rather than merely pointing up contradictions between the faith of Christians and their actual practice of it, it may be more apropos to the intent of this particular issue of *Concilium* to speak of actual approaches being taken with regard to the general problem. I would like to start with a particular situation, ours here in the Philippines, and from it proceed to what could be of more universal application and relevance.

2. FACING UP TO THE PROBLEM

Barely two years ago, in November 1977, a little but nonetheless historic three-day meeting took place in Davao City on the island of Mindanao, Philippines. In attendance were some fifty Church workers from all over the country in what was then called 'the Cultural Communities Apostolate': two bishops, a dozen or so priests and religious, a greater number of lay men and women. It was the first nationwide meeting ever called by the Church of the Philippines, more specifically the Episcopal Commission for Cultural Communities, to assess and re-direct its work among the ethnic minorities of the nation.

A number of decisions was taken at the meeting, but to my mind the two pivotal ones were (1) the change of the Commission's (and the apostolate's) name from that of 'Cultural Communities' to 'Tribal Filipinos'; and (2) the adoption of a 'philosophy of work' of Church personnel labouring among the various tribal groups. These two specific decisions, needless to say, have plenty to do with the general theme of this issue—the dignity of those without dignity—and with what has already been said about the active assertion of people's 'lost' dignity.

3. THE ETHNIC QUESTION IN THE PHILIPPINES

It is impossible in the space allotted to give even a brief history of the ethnic question in the Philippines, necessary though its telling is to a proper understanding of the problems involved. Suffice it to say that in Philippine society today there is a rather clear-cut division between Christian and non-Christian groups dating all the way back to Spanish colonial times—to Spanish policies, in fact, of conquest and Chris-tianisation. The subjugated tribes (today 90 per cent of the total popu-lation of forty-five millions) became the Christian peoples of the Philip-pines, and they became hispanicised, not to the same degree and extent as Spanish-dominated and -miscegenated Latin America, but enough to make a difference; the unconquered tribes, on the other hand, both Muslim and animist (the remaining 10 per cent), have stubbornly clung to their pre-Spanish traditions, and this too has made a difference not only in the religious sphere but in the political and economic as well.

The division has shaped up, in the course of its evolution, into a classic Marxist scenario: exploiters against exploited, oppressors against oppressed. Under the present political set-up of a military dictatorship, it is at its explosive worst. The old laws and provisions in the Philippine Constitution that gave at least paper protection to the rights of ethnic minorities are no longer in force under the rubric of national security and economic development, and as a result, the minority tribes are now more vulnerable than ever before. A good many grandiose development pro-jects (dams, especially, for electricity and irrigation projects, mining, and lumber industries, etc.) are being pushed through in areas traditionally occupied by ethnic groups without much regard for their aboriginal rights to their lands and with no real provisions—though there are promises galore—for adequate compensation.

To say thus that the over-all result of current government policies toward ethnic minorities is the loss of their ancestral homes, the des-truction of old ways of life, psychological and physical insecurity, degra-dation and even genocide, is simply to belabour the obvious. It is in the perspective of these developments, both historical and cultural in general and the most recent in particular, that those two simple but truly momentous decisions of the Church workers' consultation in Davao must be viewed.

4. TRIBAL FILIPINOS

'What is in a name?' It is easy to dismiss as a futile at worst, or at best an inconsequential, act of bravado the deliberate adoption by the ECTF (Episcopal Commission for Tribal Filipinos) of the term 'tribal', a pejora-tive one in the Philippine context, to henceforth identify the ethnic minorities of the nation. But what is at stake here is the pride of people, their dignity, their very identity. Behind the choice of the name is a whole history of misunderstanding, contumely, neglect, outright oppression, and in recent years the danger and reality of further debasement and eventual extermination. Now there is a growing realisation among many tribal groups, born of desperation in many cases, of the truth of what this paper has started out with as one of its main theses, to wit, that their violated dignity and the rights that go with it will not be recognised or defended unless they themselves act to assert them, problematic though the very asserting is under prevailing conditions of military rule.

It should be noted here that the adoption of the name was not made by 'Christian' do-gooders, foreign or native, but by the 'tribals' themselves. More than half of those at the consultation were members of ethnic groups, and it was at their initiative and insistence that the change was made. The open acceptance of a name of shame to describe themselves was the first step in the assertion of their people's dignity, in essence a deliberate effort to transform a source of insult and approbrium into one of honour and pride.

5. PHILOSOPHY OF WORK

Important as the choice of a name was, the hammering out of a philosophy of work was of even more crucial consequence. The text of the declaration reads in full:

> We affirm the God-given dignity of the Tribal Filipinos and their cultures. They are our equals. We respect them.
>
> Our evangelisation is a witness of life and humble service. We offer Christ's Message of Salvation to them in a dialogue of life and faith with them, as a gift and an invitation which they can receive and respond to freely in their own way, in their own time.
>
> This humble service imposes on us a continuing process of: (a) analysis of our own and each other's culture; (b) appreciation of our mutually enriching cultures; and (c) a cultural synthesis, that is, the growing together towards a national identity of self-determining partners.
>
> Alone, each culture, because of its inherent weaknesses, is vulnerable to the exploitative forces of society; but, united as friends, we find our strength in the assurance that each is willing 'to lay down his life for his friends'.
>
> We therefore pledge ourselves to the building up of interdependent yet self-determining communities through:
>
> 1. Participation in the Tribal Filipinos' opposition to all attempts to destroy their cultural heritage;
> 2. Participation in their opposition to all forms of exploitation and violation of justice and human rights;
> 3. Sharing resources in the promotion of liberating education and organisation.

The 'philosophy of work', taken in its historical context, speaks eloquently for itself and needs no further explanation beyond the fact that it is the articulation of a way of thinking that has been developing in the minds of many workers—lay, clerical, religious, foreign as well as native—ever since Vatican II burst on the 'missionary' scene with its seminal ideals on a more open and responsive Church. But if it is a way of thinking, it is also a way of doing in the Philippine Church's apostolate to Tribal Filipinos, in fine, a revolutionary re-directing of the Church's mission to the nation's tribal peoples.

6. REFLECTIONS ON THE ECTF APPROACH

There are many points that can and must be made about the approach to evangelisation—in the final analysis it *is* evangelisation we are talking of here—that the ECTF has been evolving these recent years. I would like to set them forth here by way of resumé, also by way of further questions on the problem of human dignity.

1. *Giving versus Taking Dignity*

Almost unconsciously, when we talk about the dignity of those without dignity, it is, as was intimated earlier, in terms of *giving* it—'restoring' it, that is—to those who by historical and other circumstances have been deprived, even robbed, of it. Rarely, if ever, do we think of the possibility of its being actively *taken* by those considered without it. The converse is also quite true: the dispossessed find it easier to think in terms of re-covering dignity from those who deny it to them, hardly in terms of asserting *what they already have*. I have the feeling that where human dignity is understood and accepted as something innate in people and not a privilege conceded by their 'betters', a great many practical difficulties with regard to the question would be avoided, even eliminated altogether. But looking at human dignity in this light—that *is* itself a great part of the problem.

2. *Criterion for the Giving/Taking of Dignity*

In the practical order, the one effective criterion by which we can tell if we do not merely talk about human dignity but really believe in it is our readiness to respect the rights of human beings *qua* human beings *as we understand and define those rights culturally*. I expressly underline the preceding phrase to undercut the specious argumentation often advanced by dictatorial governments to support their blatant violations of human rights, to wit, that the concepts of human rights and human dignity and the concern for them are Western inventions and obsessions which cannot be applied to peoples and nations of other cultural traditions. The unavoidable truth is, however, that when one gets through to the core of things, what are ordinarily proposed as 'universal human rights' are in truth *rights, human*, and *universal*. Their precise manifestation, the degree of emphasis put on them, the emotional affect accorded them—

these are all culturally nuanced, but in essence the rights themselves differ little from culture to culture.

3. *The Politics of Confrontation*

When people stand up for their rights and thus assert their dignity as free agents of their good, inevitably they come into conflict with political and other vested interests. And the whole enterprise that goes under the rubric of defence of human rights and the dignity of people becomes imbued with a political cast that, though not entirely alien to it, nonetheless vitiates its primarily human and humanising character. There will necessarily be conflict—so long as there are people who find the denial of rights to fellow humans profitable to themselves and are unwilling for that reason to grant others recognition of those same rights; so long too as there are among those deprived of their rights and dignity men and women who are determined not to endure further degradation of themselves as people and are ready, whatever the cost, to affirm their dignity. The conflict is inevitable. The problem is how to resolve it in a human and Christian way.

4. *The Conscientisation/Organisation Ethic*

The politics (or mentality?) of confrontation does not necessarily nor even ordinarily lead to violence. It is amazing how the disenfranchised and downtrodden, in a heightened state of awareness of their oppressed condition, do not, as the established are wont to believe, turn their thoughts as a matter of course immediately along lines of violence. Not that the temptation is not there, alluring, enticing, at times even purposely promoted by some Church workers not a little enamoured with ideologies of violence. But left to their own good sense, people will opt to act and organise on their own behalf in a peaceful but nevertheless effective way. This is the ethic of the conscientisation/organisation approach we are talking of here, and it is precisely its non-violent aspect, implied more often than explicit, that scares right-wing governments out of their wits and impels them to raise their usual hue and cry about 'communism, subversion, rebellion'. Violence they can handle with equal violence. But the non-violence of the defenceless and the weak—they must turn it somehow into violence, even if only in name, in order to be able to cope with it on the flimsy pretext of national security.

5. *Basic Communities*

The ethic will work best in a community of men and women who in mutual trust and concern will sit down and reason together in order to act together for the common good, ever searching for ways and means to create within their capabilities an ever more human society in which collective and individual rights will be truly honoured. The dialogic character of basic communities cannot be stressed enough. The demands that are inherent in the concepts of human dignity and rights and their implications for day-to-day living are best met realistically at the level of face-to-face interaction. And concomitant with this interaction is constant discernment and reflective analysis by the entire community on their life problems and *their* solutions to them. The wide-awake readiness to confront problems together is all part of that ethic we spoke of above but now set in the context of basic communities.

7. THE CHURCH'S TASK

The five points briefly touched on above may or may not adequately say all there is to be said about the ECTF approach to what are in actuality its main objectives, namely, (*a*) the inspiriting of ethnic minorities to a renewed sense of their dignity and uniqueness as people, and (*b*) the educating of majority groups out of their age-old prejudices against Tribal Filipinos to more decidedly Christian outlooks and values. These objectives are nowhere explicitly stated in the 'philosophy of work', but they are there, unspoken but loud and clear as thunder.

It is these objectives—more than the approach itself, I should think—that raise the really significant questions about the Church's task of evangelisation with regard to tribal minorities and the concern for their diminished dignity. For when one goes to the heart of the matter, they do, one finds out, pose the following hard questions:

1. Are we as Church concerned for the dignity of ethnic minorities merely because we seek, ultimately, their conversion to institutional Christianity?
2. Or because, in view of our rather spotty record in the past, we now wish to be more credible witnesses to the Gospel by living up more faithfully to its demands in regard to human dignity and rights?
3. Or, finally, because we believe helping to save, preserve, enhance the dignity—and therefore the very humanity—of people, of 'the least of His brethren' especially, is, regardless of any considerations of conversion or witness, a pre-eminently Christly task and this by itself is justification enough for our involvement in it?

The questions are by no means academic. And neither are the answers. For on them depends *whether* and *how* we will affirm or negate our own dignity as Children of the Father.

Mariasusai Dhavamony

Christianity and Societies Based on a System of Caste (e.g., India)

1. DEFINITION OF THE CASTE SYSTEM

THE caste system in India is a complex phenomenon, closely linked with Indian social, economic, political and religious institutions. The problem of 'backward classes' or 'schedule castes' has arisen chiefly from the caste structure of the Hindu society. In order therefore to understand accurately the relationship between Christianity and the caste system, it is necessary to give a brief sketch of the caste system in its different aspects. A caste is an endogamous group or groups, with a common name, whose members follow a single or many cognate occupations, claim a common origin, and form a homogenous unit, more closely allied to one another than to any other section of the society in which they live.[1] Caste (*jati*) is a later development of, and distinct from, a much earlier system of four classes (*caturvarna*) of the ancient Hindu society: Brahman, Kshatriya, Vaishya and Śudra, whose functions were different; the Brahman's duty was to study, teach and interpret the sacred writings, and to perform sacrifice for the benefit of the community; the Kshatriya's duty was to protect the people by proper government and administration; the Vaishya had to undertake business and cultivate land, whereas the Śudra had to render service to the other three classes. But caste is a subdivision of these different classes, and this subdivision itself admits many other subdivisions, possessing superior or inferior status with respect to other such divisions.

There are various elements that constitute the caste system proper.[2] First, caste implies the idea of hereditary specialisation. The son of a blacksmith will be a blacksmith and the son of a warrior will be a warrior whether he is competent or not, whether he wishes or not. To perform the family occupation is not only a right but a duty imposed on the children. Second, caste supposes a hierarchy, inequality, with unequally divided rights and privileges. Personal status for life is determined by the rank of the group to which one belongs. Third, caste implies codified social distance and ritual ranking of society. Each caste group is closed in itself without social relations with other groups regarding marriage or food habits, considering the contact of the 'stranger' as impure and degrading. There are different explanations of the origin and growth of the caste system: religious motive, functional division of society, racial factors, custom and usage, tradition and tribal divisions, etc. A number of these factors has contributed to it at various intervals with varying emphasis on one or the other.

Is the caste system peculiar only to India or universal and common to all civilisations? How is this related to analogous social institutions such as guild, clan and class? Stratification of society is found even in the developed countries of the world. Social distinctions and social distance do exist in all societies. Even in democratic societies egalitarian ideology holds good in theory and before the law but in actual practice inequality appears an accepted social fact: namely, inequality in income, wealth, social prestige, social standing, political power, etc.

The social stratification in India is, however, based on heredity, i.e., birth, rather than on individuality and thus becomes distinctively a caste system. Another trait that distinguishes the caste system is that it is all-comprehensive and regulates not only the vocational set-up but also the moral and religious behaviour, with the social injunction that those of the group who fail to observe caste rules become out-castes. Besides, the practice of 'untouchability' based on ceremonial purity is a peculiar characteristic of the caste system. We have to note that during the course of long Indian history caste held together the fabric of society and that people opted for social security and solidarity rather than for equality. The lower castes were convinced that one can attain perfection by doing one's own caste duties well and by remaining withing the fold of his own caste. The performance of one's own duties was deemed more important than the demand for rights and privileges. The sense of unity and social harmony became the norm of one's conduct. This explains why the caste system lasted for such a long time in India. But the perverted aspects of the whole caste system were the following: the rigid concept of social hierarchy, the theory and practice of pollution, birth as the determinant for the selection of occupations, and static social structure. As A. R. Wadia justly points out, 'Worst of all, she (India) has become the home of untouchability and unapproachability which have branded her with the curse of Cain'.[3] The theory and practice of pollution assumed such great proportion as to consider the touch and even sight of the untouchables as polluting: so much so that the untouchables were deprived of all services of the community such as the use of public wells, entry to temples, schools, medical aid, and other facilities, for fear of contamination.

2. CRITICISM OF THE CASTE SYSTEM WITHIN THE HINDU FOLD

Within Hindu society itself, not to speak of Buddhists or Jain, these were strong movements against the ideas of caste discrimination and social exclusiveness. The reform movements advocated the value of universal brotherhood, rationality, liberalism, and the concept of equality and justice. The great South Indian Vaishnava and Śaiva bhaktas (God-lovers) repudiated the caste system and preached the message of universal brotherhood and unity of the human race based on the Fatherhood of God. Not only the great Hindu reform movements like Brahmo-samāj, Ārya-samāj, Prārthana-samāj and the Ramakrishna Mission, but also the universalisation of education by the British, the rapid industrialisation of the country, and the anti-brahmin movement in Southern India contributed to a great extent to the gradual casting off of the domination of the caste Hindus. By and by, change of social status from one to another came about among the non-brahmins, although birth was the sole criterion for classifying the brahmins. There was also a gradual tendency among lower castes to attribute brahmanhood to their caste groups for purposes of social superiority. Such a tendency is visible even today and has been called by M. N. Srinivas as 'sanskritisation' which means 'cultural and structural changes in society'.[4] The brahmins are becoming more and more Westernised and the lower castes are aspiring to be sanskritised, which means a preliminary step to Westernisation. Economic advance, practical leadership and education are some of the factors of sanskritisation but this does not always imply higher status for the sanskritised caste, as is clearly shown by the still existing untouchables. Above all, it is M. K. Gandhi who vigorously set about abolishing the caste system. He said: 'Caste had nothing to do with religion . . . I do know that it is harmful both to spiritual and natural growth. Varna (classes of society) and ashrama (stages of life) are institutions which have nothing to do with castes. The law of varna teaches us that we have, each one of us, to earn our bread by following the ancestral calling. It defines not our rights but our duties. It necessarily has reference to callings that are conducive to the welfare of humanity and to no other. . . . It also follows that there is no calling too low and none too high. All are good, lawful, and absolutely equal in status. The calling of a brahmana (spiritual-spiritual teacher) and a scavenger are equal and their due performance carries equal merit before God and at one time seems to have carried identical reward before men. . . . The essence of Hinduism is contained in its enunciation of one and only God as Truth and its bold acceptance of ahimsa (non-violence) as the law of the human family.'[5] 'Hinduism that is responsible for the doctrine of the caste is also responsible for the inculcation of the essential brotherhood, not merely of man but even of all that lives.'[6] Another outstanding personality who championed the cause of untouchables is B. R. Ambedkar. He forcefully stated: 'In a changing society there must be a constant re-evaluation of old values and the Hindus must realise that if there must be a standard to measure the act of men, there must also be readiness to revise these standards.'[7] He vowed to do away with untouchability and social injustice created by it.

The next phase in the radical change of the caste system started with the framing of the Indian Constitution.[8] Independent India has realised that freedom should be shared equally by all sections of society. All citizens are equal, irrespective of caste affiliations. Radical social economic changes must be effected to off-set the imbalance caused by the caste system. This aim is reflected in the Preamble to the Constitution of India:

Justice, social, economic and political;
Liberty of thought, expression, belief, faith and worship;
Equality of status and of opportunity;
    and to promote among them all,
Fraternity assuring the dignity of the individual and the unity of the
Nation.

Justice is taken in two senses: as representing the faithful realisation of existing law against any arbitrary infraction of it, and as representing the ideal element which the law tends to subserve. Liberty is understood as affirmation by an individual or group of his or its own essence. It means freedom, the negation of licence. Equality means an equal treatment of citizens in the enjoyment of rights. Fraternity implies human values by respecting the dignity of the human person. Article 19 deals with the freedoms granted by the Constitution; article 14 assures equality; and article 17 which refers to the abolition of untouchability illustrates the concept of fraternity. Analysing the actual situation we have to note that, although the restrictions of caste have been relaxed among educated classes and in cities and towns, they are still observed by the rural masses which account for the majority of the population.

3. CHRISTIANS AND THE CASTE SYSTEM

In every civilisation there are certain elements which are clearly inconsistent with essentially Christian principles. In Indian life and thought, the caste structure is distinctively non-Christian. To what extent do enlightened Indian Christians make efforts to remove the features of the caste system, inspired by Christian faith? To an enlightened Catholic, the caste system is not only an obstacle to social progress but it is contrary to Christian ethical principles. Besides, caste is contrary to the will of God. The brotherhood of all men follows from the Fatherhood of God, revealed in the life and teaching of Christ. The value of each human soul is absolute and not relative to social status.

As remarked above, there had been much criticism and incitement to non-conformity to caste regulations before the Christian influence was brought to bear on India. The teaching of the Buddha, the record of the Hindu bhaktas and seers contains much that is inconsistent with caste. The dominant idea of the Hindu saints was not so much one of social equality of all men as of the equality of worshippers in the sight of God; its basic principle was that by faith and virtuous living all castes became equally pure. There is much in fact in the caste system against which the dominant tolerance and sensitive conscience of the Hindus naturally reacted. It was these characteristics that made the social teaching of the gospels so attractive to the Hindus, leading the education of them to search their own scriptures for similar teaching, as in the case with Gandhi. It is also striking that they were concerned only with practical and social needs and with the emotional side of ethical problems, so that they failed to connect the social teaching and practice of Christ with his essentially religious teaching or with the theological interpretation of his life. Nor did they seek to find whether the ethical principles were equally dependent on and bound up with the religious tenets of Christian orthodox belief. It may be true that caste does not owe its origin to religion but it acquired a religious sanction in the course of time. Besides, caste is admittedly connected with the Hindu doctrine of *karma* and the belief that social status is determined by the nature of man's life in his previous existence, still persists. A man's duty (*dharma*) in life is to conform with the rules and standards of his caste. But a modern Hindu like Radhakrishnan will argue that though the caste system has degenerated into an instrument of oppression and intolerance and tends to perpetuate inequality and develops the spirit of exclusiveness, these unfortunate effects are not the central motives of the system.

The only legislative enactment which had had a direct bearing on the caste system is the Caste Disabilities Removal Act (XXI of 1850) which ruled that any law or usage which inflicted forfeiture of rights or property, or which might be held to affect any right of inheritance, by reason of anyone being deprived of caste should not be enforceable in the courts of law in British India. This act was intended to protect converts either to Christianity or Islam from forfeiting rights in consequence of change of creed. It merely prevented any civil or legal disability being attached to those who lost their caste on conversion, and did not affect those who remained in caste. The vast majority of converts have come from the lower castes, chiefly the depressed castes known as untouchables.

The Protestant missions required converts to abjure caste; i.e., to change their social system at the same time as they changed their religion. The Syrian or Roman Catholic Church did not demand the complete abolition of caste distinctions though customs which savour of idolatry were banned. The caste system was not proscribed by the Lutheran and Anglican Churches before 1833. The Lutheran Church viewed that the caste distinctions observed by its converts were of a civil rather than a religious character, and ensured for the higher castes respect in their own community and influence among their Hindu neighbours. The same opinion was held by Bishop Heber who said that the principle, 'For meat and drink destroy not him for whom Christ died', was to be followed in the matter of meals and social intercourse. Bishop Daniel Wilson held the opposite view that the Church of England could not tolerate a system which condemned the lower castes to perpetual abasement, which was a barrier against social uplift and bonds of human fellowship and prevented Christian love. Other Protestant Churches followed the same line, holding that the caste system is opposed to the commandment, 'Thou shalt love thy neighbour as thyself'.

4. THE PRESENT SITUATION

However, the complete change in social life, involved in the repudiation of caste, has been an obstacle to conversion to Christianity, it also deters many who would otherwise confess the Christian faith from receiving baptism. On the other hand allowance of caste distinctions within the Christian community even solely at the social level has made it less homogeneous, divided as it is into castes and parties, mutually exclusive and discriminatory. The depressed classes or the untouchables have less objection to renouncing Hinduism and embracing Christianity because by so doing they acquire a higher status and in many places they cease to be regarded as untouchables by their Hindu neighbours. And yet within the Christian community something like the caste group consciousness has developed, creating group vested interests and power struggles within it and threatening the true sense of Christian fellowship. What we have within the Church is not the original caste grouping, but a strange mixture of consciousness of cultural traditions, language, native place, social origin, regional loyalty. It is in this sense that the Syrian Christians of Kerala form a group, distinct from the Pulaya Christians; the Nadars claim to be a separate Christian group as against the Vellalas in Tamilnadu; and the Malas differentiated from the Madigas in Andhra Pradesh.[10] The Kerala Christians are divided into a number of groups such as Chaldean Syrians, Jacobite Syrians, Latin Catholics, Marthomite Syrians, Syrian Catholics and Protestants. Each of these groups tend to practise endogamy. Among the Catholics themselves the Syrian Romans and the Latin Romans generally do not inter-marry; similarly between the Marthomites and the Jacobites.[11]

An important development among the Pulaya Christians of Travancore is the emergence of the Pratyaksha Raksha Daiva Sabha (PRDS), God's Church of Visible Salvation, founded in the 1930s by the late Poykayil Johannan, a Pulaya convert to Christianity. First a Marthomite, he joined the Brother Mission where he proclaimed that caste differences should be abolished. When it was proposed to marry a Syrian Christian girl to a Pulaya Christian youth and the local Christians threatened severe sanctions, the inter-caste marriage was abandoned. As a consequence Johannan formed the PRDS with a majority of untouchables and a few Syrian Christians. He was acclaimed as the Saviour of the untouchables. He abolished the observance of caste distinctions within PRDS and advocated inter-caste marriages.[12] Similar phenomena have occurred in Kerala and other places in India and this fact brings out clearly the resentment of the Christian untouchables to the caste distinctions within the Church.

The Guntur Consultation reported:[13] 'The caste feeling within the Christian community has been somewhat overcome by the small minority of urban Christians but within the rural Christian community caste feelings are strong between Malas and Madigas, and between both these groups of Harijan Christians and Christians with a higher caste background.' The following factors were pointed out, which appear to foster the spirit of 'caste' in the Christian community:

 (i) The existence of caste from time immemorial as a hierarchical institution in India, and its adverse influence on reformist movements, both Christian and non-Christian.
 (ii) The wooing of Christians belonging to different caste groups by rival castes and sometimes by rival political parties.
 (iii) The unhappy phenomenon of some educated Christians who make use of caste for purposes of election, instead of condemning it.
 (iv) Denominational differences which have reinforced caste distinctions in places where two or more denominations are present in the same village.

5. CONCLUSION

In villages where all Christians belong to one particular caste, there is no caste problem within the Christian community. But where there are inter-caste groups in the same village, 'caste' prejudices manifest themselves in subtle forms. Theoretically and officially the practice of 'caste' distinctions is repudiated as un-Christian by all the Churches today. But in the actual life which depends so much, at least from the social point of view, on factors which are beyond the control of the Church authorities, namely differences in culture, tradition, economic and regional background, 'caste' appears to be tolerated as a lesser evil, though every effort on the part of the Indian Church is made to eradicate the evil of the caste system.

Notes

1. *Encyclopedia Britannica* IV (1910).

2. Célestin Bouglé *Essays on the Caste System* trans. D. F. Pocock (Cambridge 1971) Introduction.

3. A. R. Wadia *Contemporary Indian Philosophy* p. 238.

4. M. N. Srinivas *Caste in Modern India* (Bombay 1962) p. 58.

5. M. K. Gandhi *Caste Must Go and the Sin of Untouchability* (Ahmedabad 1964) pp. 10-11.

6. *Ibid.* p. 13.

7. B. R. Ambenkar *Annihilation of Caste* (Bombay 1937) p. 80.

8. See Ratna G. Revanker *The Indian Constitution. A Case Study of Backward Classes* (Rutherford 1971).

9. P. N. F. Young and A. Ferrers *India in Conflict* (1920) p. 134.

10. See the editorial in *Religion and Society* (Sept. 1958).

11. A. P. Barnabas and S. C. Mehta *Caste in Changing India* (New Delhi 1965) pp. 266 ff.

12. See Michael Maher *The Untouchables in Contemporary India* (Tuscon 1972) pp. 136 f.

13. See *Religion and Society* (Sept. 1978) p. 81.

Gianfausto Rosoli and Lydio F. Tomasi

The Attitude of Rich Western Christian Societies toward Immigrants

1. INTRODUCTORY REMARKS

SINCE antiquity, human migration and the international movements of peoples have been a recurrent phenomenon. Originally, transients were accepted and welcomed as 'pilgrims' or 'guests' within the receiving communities. Contemporary migration, however, because of its size and specific socio-economic motivations, has given rise to considerable problems within the receiving communities. Consequent on this alteration in the perception of migrants, the Catholic Church has been confronted with a historically unprecedented responsibility for the Christian development of its members within a culturally pluralistic ministry.

Since the 1800s, the stages of the industrial revolution produced various waves or migratory influxes in the Western European countries as surplus manpower was released from agriculture. Concomitantly, however, various forms of nationalism had begun to flourish throughout Europe, accentuating conflicts in interethnic relationships. Labour migration during this period conditioned by the national level of economic development, functioned to displace poor workers, especially farmers, to more advanced or developing economies. Thus, human mobility, as it became associated with huge migratory movements, has been forced mobility, which has seldom been considered, at least during the early phase of migration, in conjunction with the social mobility of the receiving host societies.

Although contemporary migration has taken on various forms (internal and international, seasonal and permanent, voluntary and forced, unskilled and professional, etc.), this paper focuses on international migration as the most important for the Western countries (i.e., North and South America, Europe and Australia).

Over the last century, the Church has followed an interesting path toward understanding and coping with those classes most affected by the migratory phenomenon. In fact, the growth of Christianity in many areas has been determined by the influx of European immigrants who settled in new countries destined to develop rapidly.

2. HISTORICAL SURVEY

The importance of migration in the process of industrial development, particularly in the Americas, is apparent. In America alone more than 55 million immigrants of different nationalities arrived from Europe between 1820-1930. Conversely, in countries of emigration, the manpower drain has been equally rapid. In a single century, Italy alone gave rise to 26 million emigrants throughout the world.

The different socio-economic backgrounds of the immigrants and the characteristics of the host societies has also conditioned the response of the Church to this phenomenon.

In socially less hostile environments, as in Latin America, the primary difficulties faced by immigrants were those of isolation and abandonment. The receiving Church, affected by a chronic scarcity of clergy, had little concern for, and was rarely able to meet the spiritual needs of immigrants. Consequently, a certain continuity of religious assistance was guaranteed by the few priests who accompanied immigrants. Whenever European immigrants were accompanied by their priests, a truly successful transplant of popular European religiosity was accomplished without interethnic tension: Germans, Italians and Poles not only erected a multitude of churches and community centres but, in a short time, they had built the foundation of the religious structures of the Latin American Church. Receiving societies in South America, ruled by liberal and mercantilistic élites utilised immigrants for economic concerns alone. As a result of the absence of a racist mentality within the context of a free and prevailing period of colonisation, a rapid integration into the host societies was more easily facilitated.

In the United States, which very soon became the most frequently chosen destination of emigrants, religious assistance to the migrants developed within a context of strained relations and ethnic tensions. With the opposition between Protestants and Catholics and the nationalistic conflicts among European immigrant groups (Irish, Germans, Poles and Italians, among others), it became necessary for Catholicism to adjust itself to a society convinced that Catholicism was irreconcilable with Americanism. In such an environment, a sense of competition between Catholics and Protestants developed which served to attract immigrants to their own faith. Protestant Churches, which were more powerful and connected with the dominant classes, accentuated a policy of immediate and complete assimilation of immigrants to the values and customs of the host society. The intransigence of the W.A.S.P. dominant group allowed a marginal socio-political role to immigrants (particularly Latin and Slav immigrant Catholics who only very slowly succeeded in reaching a higher social status). Consequently, the Americanisation of the Catholic Church legitimised its role in the receiving country. In this context, numerous national parishes were created by the Catholic Church to assist various national groups and a Catholic school system was established. In short, a widespread structure was developed which stands today as the most tangible sign of the growth of the Catholic Church in the United States. The urban concentration of immigrants to specific areas (for instance, Little Italies and Polonias) was the natural consequence of this marginalisation. The low level of education of these immigrants required a special assistance on the part of the clergy of the same origin.

By the late 1880s, the North European countries, in their efforts toward a large-scale industrialisation, began to attract abundant foreign manpower. The social protection of these largely seasonal immigrants, who were mostly Southern European in origin and their religious assistance was made more difficult by the strong nationalistic attitudes prevalent in the receiving countries. In spite of these difficulties and suspicions, a process of organised assistance was initiated for migrants within Europe through the international co-operation of private organisations (Werthmann-Bonomelli). The commitment of the local church to these immigrant groups varied according to countries. Yet, regardless of the comparative degree of assistance offered, local churches were invariably limited in regard to the needs of migrants (as in Switzerland and in France). In Europe, however, the deepest concern was shown by the Churches of origin which sent numerous priests to assist immigrants. With this religious assistance they also launched efforts for the social and political assistance of the migrants. The German St Raphael Society for example, was established in 1871 and followed by analogous associations in Italy and in Belgium; a religious congregation was founded in 1887 by G. B. Scalabrini, Bishop of Piacenza to assist overseas Italian immigrants; and Bishop Bonomelli developed in 1900 a lay-religious organisation (Opera Bonomelli) to assist Italian workers in Europe. Later other congregations were established for the assistance of Polish and Maltese emigrants.

From the beginning of mass migration, the Holy See was concerned with this phenomenon and assured that the Churches in the sending and receiving countries adverted to the needs of the migrants. The directives of the Holy See were numerous in this field and repeatedly urged the Churches in the receiving countries to offer adequate services to migrants, by opening the doors of their churches to them, by presenting the sacraments in the native language of the migrant, and by favouring specialised institutions such as national parishes to be used by the faithful of the same nationality and language beyond any parochial boundary. The commitment of the Holy See to the preservation of the faith of its Catholic migrant may be said to be equal to its commitment to the propagation of the faith.

In spite of urbanisation, which has characterised the experience of many immigrants, the churches and their institutions have served as a focal point for each immigrant group, allowing the survival of many ethnic institutions and favouring a true linguistic and cultural pluralism within the receiving Church. This has resulted in a richer and consequently more diversified Church. Religious orders and congregations, both male and female, were the leading forces in the assistance of immigrants, and stimulated the concern of the secular clergy.

The period between the two World Wars has characterised by restrictionist immigration policies on the part of various countries. Emigration began again, however, with greater intensity after World War II, affecting not only the traditional countries of emigration, but also the continents of Africa, Asia and Latin America.

3. TRENDS AND CHARACTERISTICS OF TODAY'S MIGRATION

After World War II, masses of European workers abandoned their regions of origin for the Americas, and later, the Northern European countries. Coupled with a process of economic and political integration, soon a dichotomy between developed and underdeveloped regions of Europe began to emerge.

In an attempt to draw a world-scale overview of migratory trends, it is easy to observe that the United States continued its restrictive and selective policy, even after the abolition of the quota system in 1965. In recent years, the most important American phenomenon is the illegal and undocumented migrants (estimated at 5 to 10 million), especially from Mexico. Since the U.S. has been historically prone to labour shortages, migrant labour there helps to maintain the rate of industrial profit by increasing the productivity of workers and decreasing the cost of labour. Illegal immigrants provide the double advantage of providing an abundance of cheap labour, because they are without legal protection.

For the first half of the 1970s, Argentina alone has been the recipient of more than 1,600,000 immigrants (6·5 per cent of the population) from Bolivia, Brazil, Chile, Paraguay and Uruguay. In Venezuela the migrant population, largely from Colombia, has been estimated at approximately 700,000. Migratory movements throughout Latin America occur mostly among rural areas and are largely neglected.

Since the beginning of the 1960s, immigration in Western Europe has increased at an unprecedented rate. This increasing trend began in the 1950s in France and Switzerland, then spread throughout Europe. It is estimated that the number of migrants legally employed in Western Europe in 1974 before the closure of the borders was about 7·5 million, comprising a foreign population of almost 12 million. At this time the total, including clandestine immigrants, may well have been as high as 13 million—a number almost equal to the population of the Netherlands. There were 3,700,000 migrant workers and family members in France; 2,800,000 in the Federal Republic of Germany; 2,000,000 in the United Kingdom; 1,000,000 in Switzerland; 520,000 in Belgium; 400,000 in Sweden; and 200,000 in the Netherlands. Migrant workers represented 8·3 per cent of the labour force in France; 8·7 per cent in the Federal Republic of Germany and no less than 20 per cent in Switzerland.

After 1974, restrictive measures were introduced and the immigrant population decreased as many migrants returned to their countries. The stocks of immigrant manpower, however, remain strong in every receiving country as a result of fertility rates. Migrant workers employed in Western Europe are presently concentrated in the manufacturing and construction sectors. In comparison to the national labour force, immigrants hold the lowest and least qualified positions. Unskilled and semi-skilled migrants account for more than 60 per cent of the total number of immigrant workers. Female migrant workers tend to concentrate in manufacturing industries (particularly textiles and clothing) and services. The majority of migrant workers in Western Europe originate from the poor regions of the Mediterranean countries unaccompanied by family. Later, depending on their adaptation and the immigration regulations, they reconstruct their families in the receiving country. The migrant population under 16 years of age was estimated some years ago in France at 860,000; 600,000 in the United Kingdom; 500,000 in the Federal Republic of Germany; and 400,000 in Switzerland.

Immigrants live in the host countries in a situation of structural marginalisation, politically (they cannot vote, except in Sweden in local elections and in other very few municipalities), socially (they do not participate in the social life), culturally (they do not read local newspapers and very few speak the language), and geographically (they tend to live in ghettos or in closed communities). Frequently, an adequate religious assistance is also lacking for immigrants.

One of the most dramatic and impressive phenomena in Europe is the phenomenon of political refugees, particularly the millions from East Europe who have been concentrating in North European countries. Forced migration, however, even in contemporary societies, results not only from political motivations, but also from economic reasons. In fact, modern emigration from Mediterranean regions toward industrialised countries is precisely a flight from conditions of underdevelopment, and a search for better conditions.

The parallel movement, then, of migration with economic development is evident and it has become more frequently recurrent and more pressingly urgent, as a key international fact in the movement of populations. The worldwide increase of illegal migration and the consequent phenomenon of trafficking manpower (black market) has demonstrated the lack of public policy in this area. Only recently have these causes of migratory phenomenon become the focus of analysis from which governments have only begun to make a united effort to study these common problems and to plan the most appropriate measures to face them.

Problems of the second generation of immigrants have also emerged after the stabilisation of migratory fluxes in Europe as it has been in the Americas. The cultural demand of the children of the immigrants is different from that of the migrant group. In addition to learning the language of the receiving country in the local school, there is the universally acknowledged need of the maintenance of the language and culture of origin.

4. WESTERN CHRISTIAN SOCIETIES AND TODAY'S IMMIGRANTS

In analysing the manner in which Christian communities dealt with immigrants, the policies of the National Episcopal Conferences and the reaction of the public and private sectors responsible for migrants must be considered.

Over the last few decades, the orientation of the receiving churches has changed to the point where immigrants have come by many to be considered as an integral part of the local community. This orientation was favoured in those countries where a process of economic and socio-political integration has been initiated (European Economic Community, European Parliament, Council of Europe, etc.).

In the aftermath of World War II, the commitment of the Holy See in the field of migration was expressed by the Apostolic Constitution *Exsul Familia* in 1952. The pontifical document collected the norms for the religious assistance of migrants, recommended Christian solidarity among Churches and stressed the right to emigrate.

At this time various Catholic initiatives, such as the International Catholic Commission of Migration of Geneva both at a national and international level, flourished.

Pope John XXIII in *Pacem in Terris* and *Mater et Magistra* linked the phenomenon of emigration to social development. He called for the equality of rights between immigrant workers and native workers and for the movement of capital rather than people. The Second Vatican Council changed once again the attitude of the Church toward migration. The question of spiritual assistance, in terms of the administration of the sacraments in the immigrants' language and the duty of a rich country to accept the displaced and poor from overcrowded areas, shifted attention to the question of international justice. The right to the maintenance of one's language and culture, and the consequent pluralism in the local community church, was reconfirmed in many documents of the Vatican Council.

In 1969 the Holy See promulgated a more comprehensive statement, *Pastoralis Migratorum Cura*, which pointed out the changed patterns of migration and pastoral needs of migrants and updated the position of the Church in line with the changes advocated by the Vatican Council. These instructions restated some general principles on the right to emigrate, the social function of all goods, and the value of pluralism. A more extensive definition of 'migrant' is also given here and a passive integration into the host society is refused. Following the principle of the collegiality of the Church, the primary responsibility was placed upon the pastors of the local churches who have the care of immigrants.

In the effort toward a central co-ordination of the various initiatives, the Pontifical Commission for the Pastoral Care of Migrants and Itinerant Peoples was established in 1970. At the national level, Episcopal Commissions on migration and executive bureaus, both national and diocesan, were created and operate in almost all countries. Starting from the most general recognition of the right to emigrate and specifying the particular rights for migrant persons, Paul VI demanded a statute for migrants in *Octogesima Adveniens* in 1971. He noted: 'It is urgently necessary for people to go beyond a narrowly nationalistic attitude in regard to immigrants and to give them a charter which will assure them the right to emigrate, favour their integration, facilitate their professional advancement and give them access to decent housing where, if such is the case, their families can join them.' In 1973, Paul VI, at the conclusion of the European Congress on Pastoral Work for Migrants, remembered that local churches are called to give their specific contribution to the solution of the problems of the immigrants.

Initiatives in those years were frequent, both in the Church of origin and in the receiving Churches. There were pastoral letters, synods, conferences and public initiatives advocating equality between native and immigrant populations and fostering an attitude of acceptance toward migrants. The Church, at this point, plays the role of a critical conscience *vis-à-vis* the larger civil society, as in the case of France in 1975, when the Church reacted to the frequent manifestations of racism and to the arbitrary expulsions by the government. Also in France the Church has begun to address an urgent ecumenical problem constituted by the large Meghrebian Community (more than 1·5 million) of Islamic religion.

In 1973, the German Synod published a document entitled, 'Foreign Workers: A Problem for the Church and Society'. The concept of *diaconia*, of service on part of the Church toward man in his social dimension, is emphasised here. Since then, almost all dioceses in Germany have issued pastoral letters and enacted specific provisions for immigrants.

The Swiss Synod in 1972 published a series of documents, which emphasised that the 'aim of the Swiss Church is the common witness in the faith and not the Switzerlandisation of the immigrants'. In 1978, the Swiss Episcopal Commission on Emigration stated that 'the Church cannot favour the rise of a marginal Christianity, but has to integrate these marginal groups into the local community'. After four popular anti-foreigner referendums in Switzerland, a popular initiative promoted recently by Catholic groups is asking for equality of treatment between natives and immigrants.

Today, in almost all North European countries, immigrants can vote and be elected in Parish Council elections, whether provided for in national law or by diocesan or parochial norms and customs. Numerous consultative organisms on migration problems exist within the Church and sometimes with the participation of migrants. These aim not only to discuss the problems of migrants, but also to assist and help them in their daily concerns.

The Church in the United States is becoming increasingly aware of the problem of illegal immigrants who are mostly Catholics and is advocating immediate action on both legal and legislative levels to remedy the situation of marginality and discrimination: 'These aliens are legally non-persons vulnerable to exploitation and prejudice here. Social assistance for employment, health care and legal protection is an important but only partial step in building the local church community. Justice within the sanctuary will not be achieved if immigrants are welcomed only on the level of case worth. An adequate response by the Church demands institutional equality and structural participation by the immigrants, as *Pastoralis Migratorum Cura* shows.' (U.S. National Conference of Catholic Bishops in 1976, Resolution on the Pastoral Concern of the Church for the People on the Move.)

In 1978, the Pontifical Commission on Emigration and Tourism issued a series of documents on the pastoral care of various types of human mobility. Finally, at the beginning of 1979, the First World Pastoral Congress on Emigration was held in the Vatican, with the participation of the newly elected pope, John Paul II. This Congress, in which numerous representatives from National Episcopal Conferences participated, was in line with the first pontifical encyclical *Redemptor Hominis*. Consequently, the Congress reiterated the rights of human persons and families to emigrate and to return 'without being subjected to political, economic, ethnic or religious pressure or violence'.

A more acute awareness of the international dimension of migration pushes the sending and receiving Churches to develop a more extensive dialogue and a more active co-operation. The new ferments of pluralism within the Church have become clear not only in an academic sense, but on the basis of the real expectancy of migrants. Within each church it becomes increasingly necessary to overcome ethnic divisiveness and to use ethno-cultural differences as valid elements of the internal dynamics within the life of the church. The specialised care to migrants should not lead to a balkanisation, but rather to an appreciation of the most appropriate instruments for the building of the local church. The welcoming of immigrants must encompass economic, cultural and spiritual aspects, fighting any form of discrimination and zenophobia. The respect of the human person and the variety of cultures are the sign of a true democracy and real pluralism within the Church.

Bibliography

For socio-demographic, historical, legislative and political analysis on international migration, see *International Migration Review* (New York 1968 to the present); *Studi emigrazione/Etudes Migration* (Rome 1964 to the present); *International Migration* (Geneva).

For pastoral and contemporary debates, see *Migration Today* (New York 1972 to the present); *Dossier Europa-emigrazione* (Rome 1975 to the present). Tomasi, Lydio F. 'The Challenge of Immigration to the American Church' *Migration Today* V (1977) 9-12.

For official documents of the Holy See on the care of migrants, see *People on the Move—Migrazioni e turismo* (Vatican City). For position of the various National Episcopal Conferences on migration, see their own publications.

For historical aspects, see Tessarolo G. ed. *The Church's Magna Carta for Migrants* (New York 1961); Linkh, R. M. *American Catholicism and European Immigrants (1900-1924)* (New York 1975); Caliaro, M. and Francesconi, M. *J. B. Scalabrini, Apostle to the Emigrants* (New York 1977); Tomas, S. M. and Stibili, E. C. *Italian-Americans and Religion; An Annotated Bibliography* (New York 1978); Rosoli, G. F. 'La Chiesa di fronte al secolare fenomeno dell'emigrazione italiana' in *Rassegna de teologia* (1979).

For some theological and pastoral reflections, see Ancel, A. *Theology of the Local Church in Relation to Migration* (New York 1974); De Certeau, M. *L'Etranger ou l'union dans la difference* (Paris 1969); Emilianos, Timiadis *Les Migrants, un défi aux eglises* (Paris 1971); De Lachaga, J. M. *Eglise particulière et minorités ethniques* (Paris 1978).

Meinrad Hebga

Worthy and Unworthy Churches

'Have you not made distinctions among yourselves?
... You have dishonoured the poor man' (James 2:4, 6)

WE are not talking here about worthiness or dignity and unworthiness or indignity in the sense of virtue or vice, but in the sense of rank and hierarchy. I might have called this article 'First and Second Class Churches'.

David Cochran wrote an article some years ago with the very suggestive title 'Churches or Missions?' and it is precisely this question that we continue to ask when confronted by the persistence of the 'theological' distinction between missions and churches in official Catholic ecclesiology. In this article, Cochran noted that Paul was successful as a missionary because he set up churches, not missions. He established native churches which, from the very beginning, had all the spiritual authority that they needed and were responsible for their own upkeep, decisions and growth.[1]

For a long time, both Catholics and Protestants had a very similar attitude towards these quasi-churches which were called missions. Since the Fourth Assembly of the World Council of Churches at Uppsala in 1968, however, the Reformed Churches have been noticeably less discriminatory even though the classical division was maintained in the Decree *Ad gentes*, on the Church's missionary activity and the Second Vatican Council made a distinction between missionary and pastoral activity in the missions and the churches respectively. To be fair, we are bound to recognise that the unity and universality of the Christian mission, which has a Trinitarian origin, are affirmed by Vatican II, which also stressed that the activities of the Church were different, not in substance, but in their circumstances (*Ad gentes*, 6). Uppsala maintained that the

Church's mission was addressed to all six continents.[2] Whereas the term 'churches of the Third World' has in recent years become much more frequently used by Reformed Christians, it is still seldom encountered in Catholic circles, despite the fact that it occurs in Saint Paul's writings and in the Apocalypse, these New Testament authors referring freely to 'churches' in the plural without fearing any danger to the unity of the body of Christ. It has, in this context, been suggested that the tendency in most schools of Catholic missiology to wish to distinguish the missions from the churches has been reflected in the conciliar decree *Ad gentes*.

1.   A FOUNDATION IN SCRIPTURE?

To put an end to any possible misunderstanding and any misinterpretation of my intention—in case it may be thought that I am, in this article, accusing those responsible for the official Catholic or Protestant ecclesiologies of racism or cultural chauvinism—I should like to say here and now that this is not what I have in mind in speaking of the distinction or discrimination made between missions and churches. This distinction is clearly the result of a sincere concern for the Christian communities that are regarded as too young to be self-sufficient. Their coming of age has been delayed because of fear that they may be left to their fate by their Western guardians and thus be deprived of indispensable personal and financial help. This concern deserves our praise and thanks. It is really the way in which it is rationalised or theoretically justified that presents us with a problem.

It may not be possible to contest an authentic conciliar text, but one is bound to express one's perplexity with regard to statements that are not at all convincing. I have already mentioned the distinction made, in *Ad gentes* 6, between missionary and pastoral activity: 'Thus missionary activity among the nations differs from pastoral activity exercised among the faithful as well as from the undertakings aimed at restoring unity among Christians.' It cannot be denied that there are different levels of growth and maturity among the Christian communities, but what did the experts responsible for this text really have in mind in contrasting a real pastoral activity among Catholics or Protestants in the older Christian countries and a simple missionary activity among the neophytes and pagans of Africa, Asia or Oceania? Did they mean that the religious education of our catechumens, the homilies, sermons and exhortations of our priests and pastors, the administration of the sacraments, the visits made to the sick, the care of the poor and so on that have taken place for decades—and even centuries, if one things of the early Portuguese colonies in Africa, for example—and are very similar to the first proclamation of the gospel or the kerygma do not form part of the pastoral ministry? I would like to express this question in a basically simple form: Was the apostolic activity of Paul, Barnabas or Silas pastoral or was it simply missionary? Did the communities founded by them belong to the noble class of churches with an authentic pastoral ministry or did they belong to the lower class of minor churches on the way towards full development?

Paul and Silas founded a church—not a mission—at Philippi in Macedonia, taught this church for a few days or at the most for a few weeks (see Acts 16:12 ff). The same happened at Thessalonica, where they established a viable community to which apostolic letters were written. This took three weeks. The communities of Corinth, Ephesus, Rome and elsewhere were also not treated by those sent by Christ as sub-churches in comparison with the mother church in Jerusalem and indeed the church in Jerusalem depended for its upkeep on the generosity of the neophyte churches. The Christians in Macedonia and Greece sent help to Jerusalem (Rom. 15:25), even though they were not rich themselves, and the apostle Paul recognised that their financial help went far beyond their means (2 Cor. 8:1ff). The gifts sent by the Philippians were a 'fragrant offering . . . pleasing to God' (Phil. 4:10 ff).

The apostles seem, moreover, to have been very flexible. If it is true that Paul was appointed as apostle of the gentiles and Peter as apostle of the Jews (Gal. 2:7 ff), this does not mean that the first confined his attention exclusively to gentiles and the second only to Jews. Peter was, for example, sent by God to convert the family of the pagan Cornelius (Acts 10:1 ff) and Paul did not miss the chance of evangelising his fellow Jews, for whose salvation he would have consented to be separated from Christ (Rom. 9:3). He made himself all things to all men (1 Cor. 9:22)—a Greek with the Greeks, a Jew with the Jews. Peter, John, Barnabas, Silas and the others were just as zealous, though perhaps they did not express themselves so freely. They too and perhaps Peter most of all had 'anxiety for all the churches' (2 Cor. 11:28). A man like Epaphras prayed fervently for the Christians of Colossi and worked hard for those in Laodicea and Hierapolis (Col. 4:12). The Bishop of Ephesus, Timothy, took the letter to the Hebrews to whom it was addressed (Heb. 13:23).

One has the impression of a free circulation of the word of God, resources and apostolic workers. In such an atmosphere of communication and sharing between brothers, the universality that is so often held up nowadays to the neophyte communities of Africa and Asia was in those days visible and credible. There was no place in the early Church for a discriminatory theology in which Catholic or Protestant churches were contrasted with missions or first-class churches were opposed to second-class churches. What is more, this theology, which is entirely without biblical foundation, would seem to have originated in special historical circumstances, those, in other words, peculiar to the political and religious structure of the apostolate at the time of the great expansion of Europe beyond its frontiers at the time of the Renaissance. I shall return to this question later in this article, because it was from this mixed source that the criteria were drawn on which the distinction between the pastoral Christian community and the missionary Christian community is based.

2. STRANGE CRITERIA

The criteria used to define a church that is worthy of the name of church are more numerical, genealogical and financial than biblical.

1. *The Statistical Criterion*

When Western Protestant or Catholic missiologists want to explain the broad difference between their churches and those of the Third World, they usually produce figures. In the West, they say, most people are Christians, at least by baptism, whereas, in the missionary countries, the majority of people are still pagans. The clergy in Europe and North America are able to carry out their tasks in their countries without resorting to foreign aid, while the people of Asia, Africa, Oceania and, to a great extent, Latin America have need and will for a long time continue to have need to call on expatriate missionaries to help them in their ministries. Johannes Schütte, who was an eminent missiologist and had at one time been superior general of the Congregation of the Divine Word, argued in precisely this way, when he pointed out that France and other Western countries, although they were undoubtedly placed in a missionary situation, had an adult and established church that was provided with all the means and the resources that were required for the task of missionising. The relationship between the mission that sent and the mission that received was, he thought, best described as that between a mother and her child. France was a missionary country, he agreed, but she had twice as many priests as the whole of Africa and Asia put together.[3]

Eugene Hillman, C.S.Sp., held the same opinion and he too stressed that France alone had as many priests and religious as Africa and Asia put together. Even in Latin America, there was one priest for every 5,000 souls, he noted, compared with only one for every 17,000 in Africa and one for every 80,000 in Asia.[4]

As Malcolm J. McVeigh has correctly pointed out, however, the Church is already established in most African, Asian and Latin American countries. What is more, if due allowance is made, there are more confessing and practising Christians in Uganda and Congo-Zaïre than in France. I would add that, apart from Poland and Yugoslavia, there are hardly any European countries with such thriving seminaries as those in missionary countries such as Tanzania, Ruanda, Uganda, Cameroon or Nigeria. There is also the question of the massive exodus of priests and male and female religious in Europe and North America, which is another important element in the very fragile nature of these theological statistics and the numerical argument as a whole.

2. The Criterion based on Age

The Western churches are very proud of their right of primogenture. If your community is young, like that of Angola and that of Congo-Zaire, which are only a few centuries old, you have to be humble and patient and remember that evangelical growth requires time. You also have to rely on the experience and wisdom of the older churches of Europe and North America. If, on the other hand, your church is situated in the Western world and can boast of a spiritual geneaology going back to one or other apostle or apostolic Father, then you automatically form part of the enviable category of Christians with a pastoral ministry. We priests and men and women religious in Africa or Asia are always ready to be asked: 'Are you a born Christian or are you a recent convert?' What does this 'born Christian' mean? Surely Jesus Christ replaced the religion of Israel which was genealogical and based on descent with a universal religion in which all are born of God and not of man (John 1:13), a religion in which there was no more right of primogeniture. God's gift is not related to age or seniority. Faith does not necessarily improve with age—it may even become duller and less vital. God may even prefer the clumsy devotion of African neophytes to the sophisticated religion of those who display their dusty archives of Christianity and holiness.

3. The Financial Criterion

Christians are realistic and believe that it is not worth setting up a diocese or a local church unless it can be shown to be financially viable. It is, however, interesting to note that Muslims have never troubled about this strange criterion, but this has not acted as a check on the vitality of Islam or its spread. Why, then, must the existence of a Christian community be tied to property, possessions and money in the bank? This is surely a characteristic of a civilisation based on money and possessions. It may not be directly contrary of the gospel, but it certainly is not derived from it. It may not be easy to escape from our enslavement to money, but it is surely possible to avoid making an appeal to reason which is not in any sense theologically sound.

3. THE ORIGINS OF THIS TEACHING

The criteria used by ecclesiologists to distinguish between 'pastoral' churches and 'missions' would therefore seem to be more sociological than theological. In view of their historical origin, one is strongly tempted to regard these criteria as ideological and political. I would not go as far as that, but it is important to recognise that these criteria are fundamentally wrong and harmful. They have perpetuated a mythical and discriminating distinction between Christ's churches and have encouraged the growth of a paternalistic, condescending and dominant attitude on the part of the 'pastoral' churches and a dependent and infantile attitude on the part of the 'missionary' churches. These attitudes have in turn led to universal statements that are made with the aim of edifying, but remain unconvincing. In addition to these two groups of criteria—the sociological and the ideological or political criteria—there is also a third tendency, which has been described as nationalistic or xenophobic. Which of these three criteria could really be called Christian without any reservation?

Clearly, we are paying the price here for a theological error that goes back to the period of the conquistadores, padroados and ecclesiologists of the European colonial tradition. It is clear that the eminent theologians of Salamanca and other Spanish universities during the sixteenth century—Dominic Soto, the terrible Sepúlveda and above all Francisco de Vitoria—provided European imperialism with a canonical theological guarantee, the disastrous effects of which can still be felt today.[5]

We should not, however, point to individual scapegoats in this, because the whole idea of Christian mission has been adulterated by the process of colonial conquest. For the first nine centuries of Christian history, the Christian faith spread throughout Europe normally in accordance with the apostolic tradition. This did not happen in the New World, in Asia or in Africa. In those parts of the world, the expansion of Christianity was essentially a process of extraversion, in which the Christian communities founded beyond the seas were no more than branches of the mother-churches in Europe or at the most distant congregations. Even when the missionary impulse came from Rome, the earlier expansion led to the establishment of autonomous native churches or 'worthy' churches. Pothinus' was such a church in Lyons. Martin and Remigius established autonomous churches in Gaul, Augustine of Canterbury did the same in England, as did Wilfrid of York. Willibrord and Boniface set up 'worthy' churches in The Netherlands and Germany and Cyril and Methodius had the same kind of churches in the Slav countries. None of these churches were conceived as dependent on religious orders or mother-churches in Asia Minor, Ireland or Greece, for example.

This was not the case in the sixteenth century and later. By virtue of the right of conquest (an attempt to limit the harm done by the exercise of this right was made in the bull *Universalis Ecclesiae* of 1598, said to be by the padroado) the Christian missionary communities were no more than fiefs of the kings of Spain and Portugal, who had sovereign power to nominate and dismiss the bishops. At the most, these communities were the private domains of religious orders and other missionary societies. This situation persisted even after the establishment of the Congregation for the Propagation of the Faith in 1622 and the publication of *Inscrutabili divinae*.

In Reformed Christianity, the distant foundations were also no more than overseas branches of the established European churches and these branches received financial help, staff and directives from Europe. The comment made by Cardinal Costantini: 'The Church's missions have been regarded as religious colonies and this has led to an attitude among missionaries which I would call territorial provincialism'[6] could equally well be applied to the Reformation. The same cardinal added that, if this spirit were to be transplanted into Italy, and Udine was, for example, made the fief of the Franciscans, Venice the fief of the Dominicans, Padua that of the Carmelites, Verona that of the Servites, Milan that of the Jesuits and Turin that of the Lazarists, none of these orders would accept 'an infiltration by members of another order' into their territory.

Those who are in power in the position of guardians are never in a hurry to take the demands made by those entrusted to their care seriously. The Church's missiologists therefore put forward their three criteria—the statistical criterion, the financial criterion and the criterion of seniority—as a means of assessing maturity in the Church, even though no trace of these criteria can be found anywhere in Scripture or in the apostolic traditions, thus leaving the way open for a distinction to be made between 'pastoral' churches and simple 'missionary' churches or between true churches and quasi-churches.

4. CONCLUSION: TOWARDS TRUE UNIVERSALITY

The biblical teaching about the unity of the mission entrusted by the Father to Christ and by Christ to his Church is beyond dispute and is common to both Catholicism and Protestantism. The ecclesiology that tends to place individual churches in a hierarchy in accordance with doubtful historical criteria of the kind outlined in this article is, on the other hand, very much open to dispute. It has made no positive contribution to the formation of a truly universalist attitude. Surely the time has come for us to cease to maintain such inconsistent distinctions by appealing to specious arguments or to authority? Would it not be better to promote multilateral exchanges, in which each Christian community could deal on an equal footing with its sister-churches, whatever their financial situation or their seniority may be? It is surely possible to break through the pattern by which there are those churches which give without receiving on the one side and those which receive, as professional beggars, without giving on the other? A new situation, in which there is an interchange of experience, resources and staff, could be created.

In such a situation, worthiness and unworthiness need no longer depend on finances or staff and could be based much more firmly on faithfulness or unfaithfulness to Christ and the church community and unity. All the members of the body of Christ could be treated with justice, respect and love. This treatment would not be reserved for those 'with gold rings an in fine clothing' (James 2:2) or for those whose churches are proud of their patriarchal seats or famous universities or are surrounded with power and glory and whose members are generally protected from abuses, repression or contempt. Why should we despair of seeing one day all the churches becoming as worthy as the poor and the humble for whom the Lord cared so much?

Translated by David Smith

Notes

1. D. R. Cochran 'Churches or Missions?' *Anglican Theological Review* (Sept. 1974) 23.

2. Uppsala Report (1968) p. 30.

3. 'Why We Engage in Mission Work' *Foundations of Mission Theology* (Jedos) 49.

4. Eugene Hillman *The Church as Mission* (London 1966).

5. Beltran de Heredia 'El maestro Domingo de Soto en la controversia de Las Casas con Sepúlveda *Ciencia Tomista*, XLV (1932) 35-49 and 177-193; Juan de Sepúlveda *Democratus Secondus, seu de Justis Belli Causis* (1550); F. de Vitoria *De Potestate Civili, De Indis Recenter Inventis, De Jure Belli* (1539).

6. Cardinal Costantini *Réforme des missions au XXe siècle* (Paris 1960) p. 45.

Part IV

The Worth of God and the Worth of the 'Worthless'

Enda McDonagh

Man and Woman are in the Image of God and We Are All Brothers and Sisters in Christ

1. WHERE IS GOD NOW?

'THE SS hung two Jewish men and a boy before the assembled inhabit-
ants of the camp. The men died quickly but the death struggle of the boy
lasted half an hour. As the boy, after a long time, was still in agony on the
rope, I heard the man cry again, "Where is God now?" And I heard a
voice within me answer, "Here he is—he is hanging here on this gallows. . . ."' (Elie Wiesel, *Night*, New York 1960, pp. 70 ff).

We need to be continuously and forcibly reminded that Golgotha is a
far cry from the beautiful liturgies and music and of our solemn
assemblies—the far cry of (near) despair at abandonment by the victim
and of disbelief by the onlookers. Where is God now? Let us see if he will
come to save him? These are questions seeking an answer from Gulag to
Robben Island, from more conventional and accessible slums and shanty
towns across Asia, Africa and Latin America. And they surface per-
sistently and acutely in millions of typical cases in the 'affluent' and
'Christian' West; cases like Chris in Dublin, homosexual, rejected by his
family, enemployed and by now unemployable; or like Liz tied to an
alcoholic husband who beats her while her six children are gradually
abandoning their impossible home and 'inadequate' parents; or like
Seamus who was picked up by the police, beaten and sentenced although
protesting his innocence is now on the 'blanket' in Long Kesh prison, i.e.,
living in his own excrement; or like Hazel whose husband, a prison
officer, was shot before her own and her daughter's eyes, or. . . . One
could go on and on listing the griefs and degradations that are all about us,

115

just around our own corner or stretching across the globe in a chain of terror and oppression that defaces and obscures the image of God in man, oppressed and oppressor, that inevitably and reasonably if often despairingly or hostilely raises the final question, 'Where is this God now?'

For the alert and alive Christians the question is both inevitable and painful. Too many of us are more alert to the pain of the question for us, than to the suffering of the boy on the gallows, so we ensure by our sleepers and tranquillisers that we are not awakened by sight or sound of suffering humankind. The defaced image of the gallows is carefully excluded by concentrating on the pretty and prettified faces with which we surround ourselves. The cries of pain from the ubiquitous torture chamber, political and domestic cannot penetrate the mediacentres we call our homes. Only the great exclusion of the degrading and disturbing enables us to enjoy life or even to survive. There are people to take care of these things. Pilate's hand-basin is invisibly at our side. Besides we pay our taxes and so contribute to all kinds of welfare projects at home and abroad. We even make voluntary contributions to several programmes designed for the needy. We are never consciously unkind to the deprived: we just don't want them around us.

So much of Western Christian living for laity and clergy seems to be bounded by the limits just described, the limits of the 'Great Exclusion'. And so much of the reflection on Christian living which in its systematic presentation we call moral theology, takes few halting steps outside these limits, that we may be faced once again with a *trahison* not just of the *clercs* but of the *croyants*. At least reflecting believers, professional theologians and others, have to consider how far the 'Great Exclusion' may be the ultimate exclusion, the exclusion of God, and how far the question of where God is now, may be more appropriately raised in the circles of the privileged than among the 'Wretched of the Earth'. At any rate there is the awkward difficulty of reconciling the God of the privileged and oppressing peoples with the God of the deprived and oppressed. For the moral theologian description and analysis of the Christian way of life must return to the life and example of Jesus, his search for and finding of God ultimately on the Cross, but along a route that took him to seek out and befriend the outcast and 'undignified' of this world, develop a community of disciples from them and then experience their betrayal and desertion at the crucial time. Rejected by the leaders, the masses and even his friends, he prayed to be spared the final indignity of criminal crucifixion and cried out as the possibility of final abandonment, suggested mockingly by his enemies, came crowding in on him. He might well have been waiting on the Godot of Becket's tramps, Didi and Gogo, but for him the only tomorrow possible was in the transformation of the Resurrection, the Father's response to Jesus in final recognition and acceptance. This person's life, death and resurrection form the heart of Christian living. They must also form the heart of Christian theology, Christians' fumbling attempts to recognise, explore and express the nature, relationships and activities of the God of Jesus Christ. To make any significant progress in this daunting task the 'Great Exclusion' which Jesus overcame in his personal relationships and most profoundly in his sufferings and death, must be in turn overcome, at least partially, by believer and theologian. The searching question about God's absence and presence must be honestly and courageously faced. Evasion of these preliminary tasks invalidates the whole exercise and with particular ignominy for the moral theologian.

2. THE IMAGE OF GOD AND MORAL THEOLOGY

The structure of the Christian life and so of moral theology might well be described as the call to unveil, discern and recognise the presence of God as he has communicated himself in the covenants of creation and incarnation. The recognition involved is no mere doffing of the hat or nod of the head to be accompanied by 'polite meaningless words'. It is a recognition that constitutes a way of life and a life's task, for the 'terrible beauty' of the living God demands total human response and is constantly in danger of being obscured by the false beauties of gods created in our own image. In so far as that moral theology is a Christian theology, its structure and method of analysis must reflect and reflect on the paradigmatic unveiling of the presence of God as it occurred in Jesus Christ. His focus of interest on the poor and the outcast and his own acceptance of the role of the suffering (and rejected even unto death) servant, provide moral theologians with an inescapable starting point in their analysis of the pursuit of God as he is mediated through his created human images and finally through his own son.

To begin one's moral theology by seeking God within the rejected and apparently deformed images of the outcast, the suffering and the handicapped poses immediate and difficult problems. How can it be reconciled with the traditional understanding of creation reflecting the *vestigia Dei* as the heavens proclaim His glory, the glory of God in humanity fully alive and the created world is charged with the grandeur of God? Whether morality is conceived in terms of the coming to fulfilment of the work of the Creator and indeed Redeemer God or in the other classical Christian tradition of the Natural Law, it seems almost perverse to attend first of all to the deformed images, the failures of creation or society, in search of the summoning, empowering and guiding presence which a theological analysis of morality might ascribe to God. It intensifies the very problem of seeing God as source and terminus of morality by underlining the very aspects of human existence, the handicap, illness and degradation, physical, mental and spiritual which constitute the difficulty of seeing God as all-powerful and yet moral or loving creator. Yet however one attempts to explain the evil in the world, at least the physically, mentally and socially and even spiritually deformed human beings may not be overlooked or excluded in any Christian contemplation and repose to the image of God in the world. If one is to take as critical the example of Jesus himself, one will turn first to these as truly mediating as well as needing God, and as ultimate test of our ability to recognise and respond to the supreme mediation of God in Jesus himself. 'As long as you did it to one of these least ones . . .' (Matt. 25).

It is important to the true recognition of their mediating role as images of the divine and to the moral value of response to them that they be recognised and respected as valuable in themselves, divinely valuable with all the dignity that goes with that, and not merely as recipients of our or even God's special care and above all not as occasions for our moral activity. The real disrespect and indignity would be to make the deprived into stepping stones for the privileged on the way to God.

3. THE UNITY OF HUMANKIND

Part of the difficulty in discerning the image and presence of God in the least ones derives from the sharp individualism which dominates our thinking. Image of God is for us to be associated exclusively with the individual. The other individual and particularly the individual with a difference which is by our standards impoverishing, is alien to us in a host of ways which may easily exclude from our consciousness and certainly from our consciousness of him or her as locus of God's presence and manifestive of God's nature and glory. When the deprived are institutionalised or living far away or even just the wrong side of the tracks the exclusion is easier and more effective. But the individualism is not overcome by attending to other individuals including deprived ones, essential as that is. A deeper shift of consciousness is demanded whereby I think primarily in inclusive 'us' terms rather than in 'me' and the 'others' terms or in an exclusive 'us' and 'them' terms. When the unity of humanity begins to be thought and felt and acted upon, the real locus of the divine image becomes evident to us, the human race as a whole, its historical members at any particular time, taken both in their irreducible individuality and in their unbreakable unity. Until that kind of image of humanity prevails, humanity as image of God will be partial and fragile. The understanding of the Church as sacrament of the unity of humankind to which Pope John Paul returns a number of times in his first encyclical *Redemptor Hominis* reflects this basic Christian truth. Each one's imaging of God and its moral implications are inseparable from the total imaging and mediating which form the origin and criterion of human dignity and indignity. The dignity of the 'undignified' cannot be separated out, leaving the dignity of the rest intact. Averting one's eyes and ears and minds from Chris or Liz, from the victims of thalidomide, poverty or torture does not eliminate their significance for one's own dignity. It merely impoverishes the meaning and living of that dignity.

4. BECOMING HUMAN

Given that it is the whole of humankind which properly reflects and mediates God according to Christian understanding, it must be further recognised that that humankind is only partially realised in any particular era or group or individual. Participation in humankind is a historical, developing and always incomplete process. In that sense no total participation is available in history even for the most gifted individual. We are all always incomplete, partial, handicapped and deprived, without of course our basic human dignity as mediating and reflecting God being destroyed. Our relativisation undermines much of the muddled thinking that colours our attitudes of superiority and inferiority. It could be easily transposed into the offensive 'There but for the grace of God, go I' or some other patronising expression and attitude. That is not the point at all. The other whom we are tempted to patronise for some supposed inferiority is equally God's gift and grace and a necessary reminder, better revelation, to us of the diversity of God's gifts and of our necessarily limited sharing in them. Lord and Lady Bountiful's slumming bears no relation to the recognition and response which characterised Jesus' behaviour; his response to the physically ill, the socially outcast and the evidently sinful from the paralytic to the publican to Mary Magdalen is our norm.

If we are not allowed slumming and do-goodery in face of conventional illness and poverty, perhaps God is; some traditional interpretation of both saw them as an opportunity for discipline and development on the human side and testing, eventual caring and love on the divine side. Both elements create difficulties. Some of the more awful physical or social suffering appears to reduce rather than enlarge the human character of the victim and its canonisation as divine test easily leads the non-victims or social agents to hypocritical resignation on behalf of the victims—a truly opiate effect. The suggestion of a sadistic God trying out his experiments even for our ultimate reward seems incompatible with the God who empties himself to assume the human condition of the suffering servant. It is precisely here that the Christian experience of God uneasily

harmonises with the all-powerful, impassible deity, remote in his trans-
cendence and apathetic if not sadistic in his experimentation.

Without presuming to offer any satisfactory, much less definitive
answer to these classical difficulties I consider that two factors, one
anthropological, the other theological, have a bearing on how we address
these difficulties. Becoming human is not just an individual but a social
task, not merely in the sense that one becomes human in community over
time but that the human condition emerged gradually and is still struggling towards some richer achievement. In that evolutionary-historical
development it is possible to observe the slow struggle towards and of the
human species in which all of us with our various gifts and limitations are
engaged. The struggle to become human, at first a strictly evolutionary
one and then a historical one, remains a permanent task with its historical
as well as its evolutionary triumphs and failures. Triumph and failure
characterise the lives of all of us, in their biological, psychological, social
and other dimensions. The 'undignified', as they appear to us, are a
critical part of that struggle, frequently in their very conventional failure
and indignity pointing the way to new possibilities and triumphs. Our
forward thrust as a human race is as much dependent on the apparent
failures as successes. This is reinforced for us in remembering that our
criteria of discrimination between genuine success and failure are so
crude, so invested with self-interest and so blinkered by the social,
cultural and personal conditions in which we are formed.

5. GOD AND THE HUMAN STRUGGLE

But where does God stand in such a struggle and how does it concern
him? What kind of God emerges from this struggle to achieve humanity?
The preposition is not carelessly invoked. The God of Christ is so inti-
mately bound up with human origins and destiny that in the struggle
towards humanity he must be both involved and discernible. For it is the
image of God which emerges as humanity emerges, to reach its cul-
mination of sonship in Jesus. Across the spectrum of human gift and
achievement broods the spirit of the living God. In the combination of gift
and achievement which issues in the struggle towards fulfilment for
individual, group and race the image of God finds its fitful, fragmentary
and partial expression. Even in the historical Jesus the expression was not
such that one could not be mistaken. Yet that historical Jesus underlined
the sources of mistake in seeking the image and realisation of God among
the powerful and successful of this world. The suffering servant has more
potential for humanity's basic task and dignity in revealing the true God
than the mighty on their thrones or the geniuses in their laboratories or
studies or studios. The God we confront, as the Creation and Resur-

rection narratives reveal, is the source of might and genius, but the crucial revelation of him occurs in failure, suffering and crucifixion. His part in humanity's struggle towards fulfilment is not primarily that of firing the pistol shot to start the race and presenting the laurel wreath at the end, to invoke Paul's image. His primary presence and involvement is in the struggle itself, taking on humanity's burden and pain, suffering with humanity through and beyond all the natural and historical failures and sufferings human flesh is heir to. It is a suffering towards and not a simple surrender to. The physical suffering engaged much of Jesus' time and energy as a healer and in his own as well as his prophetic predecessors' message and example the sufferings of the oppressed cry to heaven for vengeance. A Christian God suffering in and with his people is not a recipe for medical or social neglect but rather a profound indictment of both. Whatever you do or do not do to these is done to this suffering God, who reigns from the gallows rather than a throne and emerges in the efforts of the paralytic to find health and yet live and love without it rather than in the success of the athlete in breaking world records. The God engaged in human struggle and suffering provides the inspiration and the power for moral response as well as the basis for human dignity even in, indeed above all, those engaged in the most difficult struggle and in the most painful suffering. The charter of the moral life which moral theologians attempt to draft for the guidance of Christians should look somewhat different if devised from the angle of suffering humanity, the angle preferred by Jesus and his God.

6. A MORAL THEOLOGY OF CARING

In the struggle towards fulfilment of a single people, each with individual, relative and sometimes complementary strengths and weaknesses, the concept of caring for one another is indispensable. Caring relationships and caring professions are cliches of the time. In that mutual caring the struggle is made meaningful as well as tolerable for many. The distinctively divine involvement finds its appropriate expression. Some clarifications and qualifications are, however, in order. The caring by the self-styled strong can easily become self-indulgent and patronising, revealing the slumming attitude or using of others for one's own goals. Caring rests on recognition and respect above all. It must involve for caring and cared a reverence for the dignity and privacy and mystery of the more vulnerable and exploited. Properly and fully the caring relationship is reciprocal and dialogical, but one party, individual, group, class or even nation, can be easily maintained in a dependent and exploited role, thereby maintaining the other in an exploiting role. This defeats the whole point of the caring relationship and frustrates the positive advance to which the human struggle is directed.

Of course in infancy and old age, in personal and social sickness, some people and groups will be more dependent and require sensitive and prolonged caring. Impatience with the effort needed may lead those providing care to take the easier course of taking the dependence as one-sided and unalterable or to press for a 'normalisation' which may not be possible. In both situations the true dignity and gifts of the 'dependent' are ignored and violated. The real dependence of the 'caring' is obscured. Human solidarity is violated. Divine engagement in the total struggle is reduced to the paternalism of the 'strong'. Until we learn our need of the Chrises and the Lizes, of the physically and mentally handicapped, of the poor and exploited classes and races and enjoy the skills required for dialogue and mutual caring as partners, we cannot hope to be effectively helpful after the manner and by the power of Jesus Christ. We thus continue to frustrate the divine design of allowing His image in human-kind to grow and be transformed into the image and participation of the only begotten Son of the Father. We are not yet in a position to proclaim our universal brotherhood and sisterhood in Christ.

7. SOLIDARITY AND MUTUAL LIBERATION

The source of our being sisters and brothers in Christ is the sharing of the human condition to the point of self-emptying which God in the person of His Son undertook. It was His definitive entry into the human struggle, His climactic expression of His solidarity with all humankind. Such solidarity is the way of human salvation, pioneered for us in Jesus, offered to us as gift and task in the concrete relationships of our lives. Evasion or rejection of that solidarity is the way of damnation, of des-truction. It cannot remain in a solidarity of good intentions, of remote benevolence or paternalistic doing good. Solidarity demands sharing, being side by side, engaged as equal partners in the night-battle. So fleeing to the suburbs or offering them cake or employing others for that kind of thing in order to escape personal involvement will not entitle us to say Lord, or validate our claims to be sons and daughters of the Father because we refuse the demanding task of being brothers and sisters of one another. Our exclusiveness becomes our exclusion. Our efforts to be free of it all or rather of them all result in our enslavement and imprisonment. We are rapidly engaged in constructing our own Long Kesh or Robben Island.

Without Jesus Christ and the God of Jesus Christ there is no salvation, no liberation. Without these least ones there is no access to Jesus and the Father. In Christian perspective we need them more than they need us. At any rate if we are the escapers and evaders we are also the rejecters of sonship and daughterhood. The solidarity of mankind illuminated and given final significance by divine engagement in its struggle, provides the way of salvation as the way of effective brotherhood. That salvation is a mutual liberation into the freedom wherewith Christ has set us free (Gal. 5:1).

8. LETTING GOD BE HIMSELF

The difficulties of understanding and accepting suffering in a creation and human life deriving from a loving God, are not entirely removed but at least easier to live with if God has shown his willingness to share them with us as he has in Christ. A fuller Christology recognises Jesus as no isolated and aberrant intervention by God to clean up the human and cosmic mess. Jesus the Christ is central to creation as well as salvation, to the cosmos as well as humanity. This engagement of God with the human struggle originates in His creative engagement with the cosmos which was created in and through Jesus Christ, the first born of all creation which is now reaching out for, struggling towards the fulfilment which is His in Resurrection. God's involvement in the cosmos and human history has taken on the character of a drama which exceeds the merely human and cosmic. It is a divine drama, in which in a sense the destiny of God is at stake. More accurately (although our expressions are all so crude in this discourse) by his work of creation-salvation God has entrusted the fulfilment of his plan to his creatures. Without their recognition and acceptance of it, in however anonymous a form, the plan cannot be fulfilled. But he did not entrust just a plan, however far-reaching, he entrusted himself. Personal relationships always involve such entrusting. God initiated personal relationships with mankind. In loving them in personal fatherhood terms he placed himself at their disposal. Would they respond as sons and daughters or not? The sacrament, effective sign and guarantee of that entrusting was Jesus Christ. What is at issue is not just the salvation of mankind but the fulfilment or betrayal of the divine trust.

In a different idiom, enjoying the authority of Jesus, what mankind has been offered by God is a share in the building of His kingdom. His involvement in the human struggle is directed towards the final achievement and the transforming fulfilment of the kingdom. The kingdom as presence of God's loving, healing and transforming power is already at work among us. But it has yet to reach its fulfilment. For that He depends on our co-operation, our solidarity with Him above all in those whom He has, through Jesus, indicated to us as primary locus of His presence, the 'undignified'. In acting out this solidarity and so promoting the kingdom we are responding to the God who is coming as well as the God who is already with us. We are preparing the way before Him. In a true sense we are letting God be Himself in His own world, with His own people. The ultimate measure of our sharing care of the neglected and rejected is the liberation of God so that He may complete His loving transformation of His world, so that He may be fully at home in it. Only when that work is completed will we no longer need to ask: Where is God now? For He will be self-evidently everywhere.

Contributors

ENZO BIANCHI was born in 1943 at Castel Boglione (Italy). He took his degree in economic sciences at the University of Turin. In 1966 he came to the village of Magnano (Vicenza) where he founded a monastic community, and began to undertake studies of the Bible in depth. He is a member of the editorial board of *Concilium* (Spirituality section), director of the spiritual biblical review *Servitium*, and also on the staff of *Bozze '79*. His publications include *Il corvo di Elia* (Turin 1972; 8th edition); *Pregare la parola* (Turin 1974, 9th edition); *Introduzione ai Salmi* (Turin 1973, 8th edition); *Salmi e cantici biblici* (Turin 1979); *Lontano da chi? Lontano da dove?—commento ai Meghillot* (Turin 1978, 3rd edition).

BERNHARD BLUMENKRANZ was born in Vienna in 1913. A historian, he holds doctorates from Basel and Paris and a diploma from the *Ecole pratique des hautes études,* where he has also taught. He now teaches at the University of Paris III and is a director of research at the *Centre national de la recherche scientifique.* He has published widely on varied aspects of Jewish-Christian relations, mainly in the patristic and medieval periods. He is president of the French commission for Jewish archives and directs the quarterly journal *Archives juives.*

FRANCISCO CLAVER, S.J., was born in 1929 and ordained priest in 1961. He has studied philosophy at Berchmans College, Cebu City, Philippines, theology at Woodstock College, U.S.A., and anthropology at the universities of Manila, Quezon City, Philippines, and Boulder, Colo., U.S.A. In 1969 he became Bishop of Malaybalay, Philippines. He is chairman of the Mindanao-Sulu Conference on Justice and Development and a member of the Episcopal Commission for Tribal Filipinos. His publications include *Sharing the Wealth and the Power: Agrarian Reform in a Southern Philippine Municipality* (Boulder 1973), *The Stones Will Cry Out: Grassroots Pastorals* (Maryknoll 1978).

MARIASUSAI DHAVAMONY, S.J., was ordained in Kurseong, India, in 1958, and is professor of Hinduism and of the history of religions at the

Gregorian University, Rome. He is a licentiate in theology, doctor of philosophy of the Gregorian University and doctor of philosophy (Oriental religions) of Oxford University. He is editor of *Studia Missionalia* and *Documenta Missionalia* and has written many books and articles.

ENRIQUE DUSSEL was born in Mendoza (Argentina) in 1934. He holds doctorates in philosophy and history, as well as a degree in theology. He is professor in the Independent University of Mexico and in the Department of Religious Studies in the Spanish American University. He presides over the Study Commission of the Church in Latin America (CEHILA), and has taken part in the Ecumenical Dialogue of Third World Theologians in Dar-es-Salaam, Accra and Sri Lanka. Professor Dussel is the author of a number of books on liberation, and on ethical and philosophical subjects, as well as a history of the Church in Latin America.

JOST ECKERT was born in 1940 in Düsseldorf. He is professor of the New Testament at the Theological Faculty of the University of Trier. His main relevant publication is *Die urchristliche Verkündigung im Streit zwischen Paulus und seinen Gegnern nach dem Galaterbrief* (Regensburg 1971).

MEINRAD P. HEBGA was born in Cameroon in 1931. He studied at the Gregorian University in Rome and later at the Sorbonne (philosophy and psychology). He is missionary professor of anthropology at the Catholic Institute in West Africa at Abidjan (Ivory Coast) and in the Gregorian University at Rome. His published works include *Les Etapes des Regroupements Africains* (Dakar 1968); *Croyance et Guérison* (Yaoundé 1973); *Emancipation d'Eglises sous Tutelles* (Paris 1976); *Dépassements* (Paris 1977); *Sorcellerie, Chimère dangereuse?* (Abidjan 1979).

ENDA McDONAGH is a priest of the Archdiocese of Tuam and professor of moral theology at Maynooth. He is currently on leave of absence as Huisking professor of theology at the University of Notre Dame. His new books, *Social Ethics and the Christian* (Manchester University Press) and *Doing the Truth: The Quest for Moral Theology* (Gill and Macmillan, Notre Dame University Press), were published in May 1979.

CHARLES PIETRI was born in Marseille in 1932 and is professor of the history of Christianity at the University of Paris-Sorbonne. He has written widely on the ancient history of Christianity and is director of the study centre founded by Henri Marrou for research into ancient Christianity and late antiquity.

LEONIDAS E. PROAÑO was born in San Antonio de Ibarra, Imbabura Province, Ecuador. He went to the lay elementary school Juan Montalvo in his native village, secondary school in the San Diego seminary in the city of Ibarra and studied philosophy and theology in the San Jose seminary in the city of Quito. He was ordained priest in 1936, became a teacher in the San Diego Seminary and together with a colleague developed the JOC and started a bookshop and newspaper called 'La Verdad'. He wrote a book called *Un metodo de Accion catolica* and a series of leaflets on the priestly vocation. On May 26, 1954, he was ordained bishop in Ibarra Cathedral and given the diocese of Ibarra on May 29. From 1960 till 1969 he was a member of CELAM As president of the CELAM pastoral department he received the job of setting up the Instituto de Pastoral Latinoamericano, which was peripatetic for some years and then set up headquarters in Quito. In his mainly poor rural diocese he set up Escuelas Radiofonicas Populares, the Centro de Estudios y Accion Social, the Instituto Tepeyac, the Hogar Santa Cruz, the Equipo Misionero Itinerante and the Instituto Diocesano de Pastoral. Since he became bishop he has written the following books: *Pour une Eglise libératrice* (Cerf), *Conscientizacion, Evangelizacion, Politica* (Sigueme) and *Creo en el hombre y en la comunidad* (Descleede Brouwer).

GIANFAUSTO ROSOLI was born in 1938. He has conducted research and written many articles on migration and at present he is the Director of the Centre for Migration Studies in Rome. His latest book is *Un secolo di emigrazione italiana: 1876-1976* (Rome 1978).

DONNA SINGLES was born in 1928 in Grand Rapids, Michigan (U.S.A.). She entered the Congregation of the Sisters of St Joseph (Kalamazoo, Michigan) and taught in schools of the congregation for seventeen years. She later studied at the *Facultés Catholiques de Lyon* (France) where she obtained a doctorate in theology in 1978 and where she is currently teaching as an assistant in dogmatic theology. She also works as *maître-assistante* at the *Institut Pastoral de l'Enseignement Religieux*.

JON SOBRINO, of Basque parentage, was born in 1938, entered the Society of Jesus in 1956 and was ordained in 1969. He holds degrees in philosophy and engineering from St Louis University, and a doctorate of theology from the Hochschule Sankt Georgen in Frankfurt. He now lectures in theology at the Central American University in San Salvador. His published books include *Christology at the Crossroads* (New York 1978).

LYDIO F. TOMASI was born in 1938 and has licentiates in philosophy and theology from the Gregorian University as well as a Ph.D, in sociology from New York University. At present he serves as the Executive Director for the Center for Migration Studies of New York, edits *Migration Today* and serves as managing editor of the *International Migration Review*. His publications include *The Ethnic Factor in the Future of Inequality* (1972), *The Italian in America: The Progressive View, 1891-1914* (1972, 1978), *In Defense of the Alien*, Vol. 1 (edited with A. T. Fragomen, New York, 1979).

Declaration of the Editorial Board of *Concilium*

CONCERNED about the ecclesial measures taken in the recent past against certain theologians and by those threatening other theologians at this moment, particularly in Europe and America, the undersigned, members of the editorial board of the international theological review *Concilium*—referring back to their previous plea for liberty in theological research within the Church, published in 1968 and bearing the names of 1,360 theologians from all over the world—would like to draw public attention to the following points:

(1) that no impersonal legal investigation procedure, but only a free and open person-to-person, believer-to-believer dialogue is capable of elucidating the theological theses of a brother in Christian faith;

(2) that the investigation procedure of the Congregation of Faith, standardised in the Motu Proprio of 15 January 1971 (AAS 63, 1971, 234-236), while offering insufficient guarantees in the case of an 'ordinary investigation', totally fails to offer any guarantee for the person involved in the case of a so-called 'extra-ordinary procedure' (the case of Father J. Pohier). For in the latter case, the errors of the author are simply assumed to be evident, without the possibility being envisaged that this evidence exists only in the opinion of the censors, and is caused by a cultural communication gap;

(3) that it is unacceptable for Rome to make unilateral decision concerning the necessity of condemning a theologian, still less so, as a consequence of the latter, concerning the taking of measures with respect to his status within the Church. Before making such decisions the Church should take account of the reactions of other theologians as well as communities, of the particular, wider or smaller public intended, of the concrete circle of readers of this author. For the process of approval or disapproval largely takes

129

place on the spot, which renders abrupt power interventions unnecessary and, moreover, harmful;

(4) we have no intention of casting doubt on the existence of a '*regula fidei*' or standard of faith, within the community of the Church, as well as a criterion for membership of the ecclesial and eucharistic community, but in the same Church there is also room for pioneer tasks (which is difficult to delineate in neat terms) destined to stimulate the developing of a contemporary understanding of Christian faith, in particular with the help of the human sciences. Therefore, we think it should be possible for people engaged in these pioneer tasks to do research freely and without being disturbed for a considerable length of time, perhaps to make errors while doing so and to be corrected by the criticism and publication of others. An abrupt intervention from above blocks these positions and the fertility of the entire process of maturing;

(5) that measures of discipline are not the right means of helping a theologian who may have made errors in certain matters to situate his point of view, neither are they a right means of helping the faithful to grasp the proper significance of a loving search for truth. For this effect, it is indispensable that account is taken, not only of the *bona fides* of the persons involved, but also of the quality of their witness of faith, rather than abstract criteria being handled as sole standard of orthodoxy;

(6) on account of all these objections, which, for the most part, also apply in the case of an ordinary investigation procedure, the undersigned think that in the case of their colleague, Edward Schillebeeckx, the church leaders, who publicly defend human rights, should also respect these rights within the Church, notably with respect to the Roman 'colloquium' to which he has been invited.

The undersigned of the Editorial Board of *Concilium*:

Professor Dr G. Alberigo
  Italy
Professor Dr G. Baum
  Canada
Professor Dr L. Boff
  Brazil
Mr A. van den Boogaard
  Netherlands
Mr P. Brand
  Netherlands

Professor Dr M.-D. Chenu
  France
Professor Dr Y. Congar
  France
Professor Dr Ch. Duquoc
  France
Professor Dr C. Floristán
  Spain
Professor Dr Cl. Geffré
  France